To HARRY
WITH BEST
WiSHES

Ruby
Goto

# GITA

### RUNNIN' DA

# SWEETMAN IZ

## COMIN'

### 'N' DA RAPPERS BE

# RHYMEIN'

### – A FOOL'S GUIDE FOR LIVIN'

## AUBU

#### MAN OF MANY MASKS

# DA SWEETMAN IZ COMIN'

Library of Congress Catalog Card Number 98-70603
ISBN 0-9663227-0-3

Manufactured in the United States of America
First Printing 1998

Published by
*JOHN L. CLARK*
New York, NY

Produced by
*PPC BOOKS*
Westport, CT

# ACKNOWLEDGEMENTS

The author acknowledges, with gratitude, the invaluable advice of
Christopher Davis (author of *Philadelphia*).

Thanks to my family and friends

Chuck Sutton, Producer, Showtime At The Apollo, and Laugh-One-Out
Comedy Syndicate, for giving me the opportunity that forced me to write.

Elder Freddy Bivens, for your wisdom.

Special thanks to my sisters Alice and Delores for always being
there............

And to all who aspire to fulfill their dreams.

# IN MEMORIAM

Georgie 1968–1997

Your smile will always be remembered!

*When the artist is alive in any person*
*No matter what his work may be,*
*He becomes interesting to other people*
*He enlightens, disturbs, upsets*
*And opens new and better ways of understanding*

—In The Art Spirit

# SPRINGTIME IN HARLEM

## THE BEGINNING

Snowflakes. The month of February, on the nineteenth day, 1934. The elements of winter waxed furious, as though angry with all nature. The frigid winds roared like verdurous beasts unleashed from the bowels of hell, boring down with relentless intent upon the hills and plains of Cumberland County, Virginia, on the night of my birth.

The winter winds of hurricane force raged through the forest that night, causing the trees to sway in frantic motion like angry hornets whose nest had been violated by a mischievous boy who had taken leave of his pubescent senses on a hot summer day, their branches ripped violently from their trunks and flung asunder like puny twigs from a sapling. Yet, in spite of the power of the storm, giant pines, maples, and birch swayed but stood like warriors in the heat of battle for their roots were anchored deep in the busom of the earth. In the sanctuary of the womb of winter, the flowers waited and dreamed of the coming of spring.

Warm spring days, birds singing, blue skies, gentle rain, flowers. Ah, the splendor of spring! The first born of the seasons. Now in the autumn of my life, once more I behold the resplendence of the Easter season and my mind drifts as though in a dream, back to Cumberland, the place of my birth. The balmy spring zephyr always brings back memories of those carefree days of my early youth. Through the windows of my mind, I see a little boy running through fields of green, chasing butterflies, and the honeysuckle growing in abundance along the sides of the red clay road, its fragrance filling the Southern air as the honey bees and insects feed with delight upon its nectar.

Fields of clover spread like plush green carpets that look as though they were woven by the skilled hand of a master carpet maker covers the undulating fields and plains of Cumberland, their pink and white buds adding the finishing touch to the masterpiece of mother nature. Warm spring days: blue skies, birds singing, gentle rain, flowers covered with butterflies and hummingbirds—hovering like celestial ballet dancers—as far as the eye can see, blooming crepe myrtle, dogwood, apple, plum, cherry, and wisteria, its vines entwined around the limbs of trees, it's lavender blossoms draped like fine silk around the limbs of a beautiful woman.

In my muse I was bathed in the memory of the effulgence of past springs, contemplating their transplendency as crystal waters flow in streams and the luminescence of the sun bathes all nature and the glow of the moon inspires song in the hearts of the night creatures and the poet. I would, if I could, remain in my present state of musing, but alas, summer approaches, and the moon flowers will soon blossom and fade, come daybreak. It has been said that spring is like youth, an over praised season.

The earth having once more awakened from its winter's slumber, Harlem is bathed in the resplendence of spring that embraces all nature like a loving mother cradling her young. It seemed as though (judge not by appearance) the world was at peace and the heart of man was made glad, after a long, cold winter sleep.

The playgrounds, parks, and basketball courts were alive with excitement. The delightful squeals of young children filled the air as they gleefully played in sand boxes and on the swings, anticipating the arrival of the Easter bunny. In the branches of the trees and shrubbery, birds mated and sang their praises to spring. Young child-mothers seated on the park benches sunned themselves in the balmy spring rays, kept an eye on their offspring, and admired each others 'weaves' as their infants sucked on their bottles and pacifiers in their strollers, undisturbed by their surroundings. On the basketball courts, shirtless young men aggressively slam-dunked the ball into the hoops, day dreaming of becoming the next Michael Jordan, as teenage girls giggled and admired the young ball players' sweaty physiques. In Mount Morris Park, the maple trees, daffodils, crocus, tulips, and Japanese cherry trees were in bloom.

Groups of men played checkers and chess. Winos in a sodden stupor panhandled for their next drink of wine. Elders, seated on benches, reminisced of times past—"Lord, things ain't what they used to be,"—and the bemused ambled about in a daze, conversing with the unseen fee-faw-fum, as drug dealers, hoodlums, hookers, hustlers, thieves, con-men, and muggers lurked on the periphery, awaiting an opportunity to strike, to ply their maleficent trades, as the police watched with a jaundiced eye. Young rappers observing the scene composed rhymes to what they saw.

# THE FORETELLER

*I*t was Good Friday and the stores on 125th Street were busy with customers shopping for their easter finery. The hair salons and beauty parlors were abuzz with chatter as the ladies were having their hair fixed, straightened, braided, and weaved. Their lips were flapping like Jay birds' beaks in a cherry tree. "Excuse me, what you say girlfriend," "Oh, no she didn't!" "I don't think so." "Don't even try it," "I know you ain't going there." Yak, yak, yakety, yak, yak went their lips, their necks moving like cobras about to do serious damage as they dished the dirt and selected false fingernails (that resembled demon's claws) of various colors, shapes, and designs to have glued to their hands. The African proprietress of The House of Hair 'n' Nails bowed and smiled profusely in spite of the cramps in her hands, brought on by the large volume of hair she had braided. Hair is big business in Harlem the year around and even more so around the holidays. One Oriental hair store, Lu Wong's Haven of Horse, Hair, Wigs 'n' Braids, was doing such a volume of business on this particular day that Ms. Wong's inventory of hair was depleted. In order not to miss a sale and disappoint a good customer, Ms. Wong cut off her own locks and sold them to a sister who bolted from the hair shop with her store-bought hair blowing in the spring breeze. "Oh I feel so white," she said as she flounced down the street.

Street vendors who sold clothes, trinkets, and food were doing a brisk business as grinning, pointing, gawking, picture-taking, tourists purchased items from them that they neither wanted or needed with the attitude of a saint bestowing a blessing upon a sinner. Some vendors appeared to be (looks can be deceiving) so appreciative of their omnipotent act of charity, they grinned and posed for the tourists who took photographs of their buffoonery. I have always despised this spectacle, but I understand its necessity and what it means to some residents of the Harlem community, due to economic circumstances and living conditions that have beset African Americans for hundreds of years in this country. Down south the elders used to say, "If you are given a bone, make a pot of soup and feed the family." Adam Clayton Powell said it another way: "What's in your hand? Use what you have in your hand."

The street was abuzz with an air of anticipation. A long line of rap music enthusiasts was working its way to the Apollo Theater's box office to purchase tickets to an upcoming "Stop the Violence Rapfest," which were selling faster than a barbecued rib sandwich. People mostly with unsmiling faces jostled each other and avoided eye contact as they move to and fro on Harlem's commercial strip. I moved gingerly so as not to brush up against anyone or otherwise come in contact with their person or they with mine. Unruly children, who resembled chocolate covered Bart Simpsons, scampered about the street bumping into and stepping on people's feet as though they belonged to them and "excuse me" was something they had never heard of. The elderly and the not so elderly bobbed, weaved, and jumped to avoid being run down by crazed looking youths on bicycles doing wheelies or being bit by pit bulls running lose without leashes, followed by their hip-hop masters, young gangstas with an attitude, child-mothers, whose breath still smelled of Carnation milk, with a 'get the fuck out of my way,' look on their faces, these young girls looking no more then two years older than the babies they aggressively pushed through the crowd in custom-made baby carriages.

Grown men urinated on the street in broad daylight and streams of piss ran down the street like water, its putrid odor, like a cloud of funk from hell, assaults the senses as it is carried up the nostrils by the spring breeze. Passerbys payed little attention and acted as though it was the most natural thing in the world. Young men swaggered with the crotch of their jeans hanging way down between their legs, with their underwear showing, a few of the bolder ones, their ass! The expressions on the faces of the elders seemed to say, "Oh God! What is this world coming to?"

A feisty old lady whacked one of the young men across his naked ass with her cane. He let out a howl. "Yo, wut up wit' dat, old lady?" "Pull yo' pants up boy 'n' cover yo' se'f, fo' you ketch yo' death o' col' in yo' hind parts, umph, umph, umph!" The young man stared at the old lady, started to say something, thought better of it, pulled up his jeans and continued down the street rubbing his back side. The balladmonger was singing the blues.

"What the hell is that?" someone exclaimed, as the relative calm of 125th Street was wrenched asunder by the most ungodly noise. Those of us who had heard it before knew that it was Mother Carye and her chickens, seven white hens, led by a black rooster, foretelling the coming of The Sweetman, the homeless pimp who meanders into Harlem on Good Friday every seven years riding on an ass (or whatever he can get his hands on), fanning himself with palm branches, heralding the coming of the second Harlem Renaissance.

Evening traffic is brought to a sudden halt as motorists pull over to the curb and get out of their automobiles to get a good view of what is causing the tintinnabulation. Onlookers' mouths drop and eyes bulge. Shoppers hurry out of stores and shops, as alarmed shopkeepers hastily shutter their stores and shops and hurry home. The chatter in the beauty parlors ceases as the ladies rush to the street with their hair in various states of undoneness. For a black woman to do this, all hell must be breaking loose.

The young mothers sunning themselves in the park hastily gather their young children and infants. The basketball players abandon their game and temporarily cease dreaming of super-stardom. The chess and checker players stop playing and the elders cease their musing of by-gone days. The drug dealers, thieves, con men and the bemused, still talking to the unseen fee-faw-fum, all rush to 125th Street as the rappers captured it all in rhyme.

Vendors hawk their wares. Greasy Pete the food vendor makes haste to stock up on an ample supply of hamburger meat, hotdogs, Italian sausages, foot longs, mayo, onions, mustard, pickles, sauerkraut, sweet relish, buns, and bread. Greasy Pete knows what's happening, seeing the large crowd gathering. Pete smelled money in the wind and made sure he was ready for the windfall.

Bill Bailey the balladmonger stopped singing the blues and put his old beat up guitar in its raggedy case and muttered, "Sweetman is back in town." Street corner preachers halted their sermonizing, political pundits, their rhetoric, which is difficult for a politician to do, and self-proclaimed philosophers stopped their postulating, and all with great haste stepped down from and hid from sight their soap boxes.

All of a sudden children and young people waxed polite. The hip-hop brothers wit' a 'tude were smiling as they leashed and muzzled their vicious dogs. People were becoming civil to each other. The tour guides from downtown, not being certain of what was occurring, frantically rounded up their sightseers and rushed them onto the tour buses to get them out of Harlem, because night was fast approaching, and back to midtown before what was about to take place transpired. The drivers of the tour buses, realizing what time it was, put the peddle to the metal, in their haste leaving some of the tourists behind. "Git yo' nigger-watching asses up outta here," yelled a disgruntled man from the crowd, voicing the sentiments of some

Harlem residents. One hundred twenty-fifth Street was becoming the scene of a great confluence of people from near and far.

"Whoaaaa...oooh...umph.... Hallelujah, Hallelujah, Hallelujah...." A hush fell upon the crowd, now numbered in the thousands. "The Sweetman is coming! Oh Glory, make way for His Sweetness," bellowed Mother Carye the foreteller, who was dressed in white from head to toe, with a red sash across her ample bosom, like those worn by church ushers. The white hens, led by the black rooster, follow her up 125th Street in a state of profuse ecstasy, frantically shaking their tambourines, crowing and cackling, foretelling the coming of The Sweetman.

Mother Carye (a stout woman) and the chickens are in a spasmodic grip of the 'spirits', and snake their necks like crazed serpents. They lunge forward, then squat low to the ground, snap upward with lightening speed, scoot backwards, and skip forward as Mother Carye trots with her arms outstretched, moving like the wings of a bald eagle gone berserk. She whirls around, stops and trembles, her body convulsing violently like a jackhammer as she feverishly strikes the tambourine against her ample thighs. "Whoo weeee.. yes, yes....behold brothers," she says, as she dances wildly. "Behold my sisters, behold lil chullin', The Sweetman is comin.' The Sweetman is comin', he who knows all 'n' sees all is a comin'."

Mother Carye, deep in an emotional world of her own, seems oblivious to the crowd. She shakes and shimmies with grace, slides from side to side, closes her eyes then opens them wide, throws her head back and moans as though she is enjoying some secret gratification. She licks her lips, moans low and groans loud, with a Tina Turner smile etched on her face. Her Cyclopean hind quarters moves faster than the wings of a Puerto Rican humming bird. "It mus' be jelly, 'cause jam don't shake like dat," a wino yells out. Mother Carye, with expression unchanged, turns to the man that made the remark and says, "Don't speak on it daddy, if you can't handle it, 'cause momma can do it easy, or she can do it ruff!" She bats her Tammy Bakker eyelashes, pouts her lips, and not missing a single beat of the tambourine, she keeps on dancing. The crowd roars with laughter. "Oh shake dat booty for me baby," yells one of the Bible-toting street preachers. Catching himself, he cups his hand over his mouth hoping no one had heard his ungodly outburst.

By now the tambourine shaking white hens, led by the black rooster, are in a hen house funk and a fowl frenzy. Frantically they flutter, cluck, cackel, and the hens laid eggs when the black cock crowed. Then they did the boogie woogie to the bus stop, 'n' did the Bus Stop as their feathers dropped, were caught up in the wind, and fell in Brooklyn, Queens, Staten Island and The Bronx (where José Ramos was smoking crack), foretelling the coming of The Sweetman. José looked up, the crack pipe fell from his lips, and he cried out, "Ay cono! Es un signo de que mierda de gallina se esta callendo del cielo. Es un signo para que me fuera a buscar ayuda." {Oh snap, chicken shit is falling from the sky. It's a sign for me to get help.}

Meanwhile, back on 125th Street, the rooster was camel-walking like James Brown. Mother Carye and the hens were in a deep state of delirium. By the time they reached the world famous Apollo Theater, still dancing wildly in a crazed state of rapture, they completely bugged 'n' went wack. Mother Carye raised her hands and troubled the wind and conjured up the muse of dance. They all started doing The Funky Chicken. The crowd joined in as they slid into, The Huckle Buck, Jitter Bug, Monkey, Dog, Charleston, Frog, Jerk, Twist, Madison, The Continental, Boogoloo, Truck, Fox Trot, 'n' what not.

Mother Carye groaning like a she elephant in heat: "Ooh, ooh, yes, yes, sock, sock, sock it to me Sweetman, umph, umph, umph." In slow motion, she bumps and grinds, like a mill grinding wheat into flour, as the sweat pours from her body into the flour turning it into dough, which she kneads with her passion, producing fluffy biscuits of love, dripping with the butter of desire. Mother Carye's head moves with serpentine rhythm, to the rhythm of Funk 'n' Fusion, which comes from an unseen source as she wiggles 'n' giggles like a precocious little girl with a naughty secret.

Unexpectedly the scene changes. Funk 'n' Fusion gave sway to gospel. Mother Carye's arms flew up over her head and she began to flail the air like a lunatic bird in flight. In the grip of evangelical ferver, shaking the tambourine frantically, she cries out, "Sweetman, Sweetman, com', com', my precious Sweetman, com'." Whirling wildly, she drops her tambourine. The strutting, prancing black rooster, his tail feathers spread like a peacock, with stealth caught Mother Carye's tambourine in his beak like a grain of corn before it hit the ground. "Don't sweat it, Big Momma, the big black cock got it. Cocka-doodle-doo, the roosters comin' through," said the rooster, striking the tambourine three times, then passing it to Mother Carye.

Organ music filled the ether. Mother Carye entered into a heightened state of sophistry, got 'happy' and began speaking in tongues. "Ya, ya, ya, eee, bellamusia, bellamonga, mellikakke, oooh, hookermasia, collardskokin, hamhocksboilin', 'n' fried chicken. "Watch that fried chicken shit," squawked one of the hens. "Sica pitbullonanigga, hogmawsandjaws, pigtrottersnkoolaid," continued Mother Carye with arms outstretched as though on a cross. She whirls and twirls, then go down on the left-hand side, bumping her left hip on the pavement. Springing up with ease, she does the Holy Dance! "Oh com', com' my Sweetman. The Sweetman is comin' to set all of yo' hypocritical asses on fire," she yells to the crowd.

Mother Carye and the chickens back away from the Apollo until they are in the middle of the street, their feet moving faster than Sammy Davis Jr.'s as they tap dance, and Mother Carye utters words that this scribe could not fathom. "Go momma Carye, go momma Carye," the crowd chants. Mother Carye's ampledge quivers like the strings on a Stradivarius violin, causing her wig to fall off. "Sister girl, yo' wig just fell off," a lady yelled to Mother Carye from the crowd. Mother Carye, annoyed, shot back, "Pick it up bitch 'n' put it on yo' ball-assed head," as she and the chickens danced up the street toward the Harlem River chanting with the multitudes joining in. "The Sweetman is comin', you better start runnin,'" and the rappers composed rhymes to what they saw.

# THE ROOSTER RAPS!

In the meantime, deep up in The Bronx José, running from the crack house, leaving his pipe behind, having beheld the vision of fowl feathers falling and fluttering from the sky through the roof, was thrown into a Fort Apache frenzy and a Bronx funk. He ran like a man possessed. Foaming at the mouth and howling like a hell hound from hell chasing a frazzled fox at a hellish pace through a forest fire to 125th Street yelling, "Yo, yo, yo, I have seen the light and shit. I ain't jivin'. I saw chicken feathers fall and shit," as he ran through the crowd addressing no one in particular. Suddenly, he found himself face to face with Mother Carye and the chickens still chanting along with the crowd, "The Sweetman is comin." José's eyes bugged further than Popeye's eyes pop when he sees a spinach patch. José flung himself at Mother Carye's feet, and she laid hands upon him. "Crack, git back in the name of The Sweetman. Demons begone. Leave this Puerto Rican alone," she commanded.

The crowd stopped chanting. Jose jumped up and hollered, "Libre, por fin, Libre por fin, Libre, por fin!" {Free at last.} He ran through the crowd towards the Apollo Theater where The Sweetman would appear, mumbling "If I can only touch the hem of Sweetman's...." The rooster spread his wings, snaked his neck, did The Funky Chicken and crowed three times. At that moment, Mother Carye stepped to the rooster and laid hands upon him also. The crowd fell silent. Mother Carye spoke in tongues. A cloud of mist, as it were, began to engulfed the rooster and the hens. As the cloud formed around them, Monks funk (Thelonius Monk), emanated from the blue and Miles (Miles Davis) and The Bird (Charlie Parker) could be heard walin' in the distance. The older people in the crowd were laid back, and began to groove to the familiar sounds from back in the day. Rabid Jazz enthusiasts donned dark shades with lips broke, ace deuce, snapped their fingers softly, and patted their feet with their head laid to the side, bobbing up and down as they sucked deeply upon a stick of reefer and waxed deeper into their groove. A hip-hoppa lamented, "Whut kinda music is dat?" "It's groovy 'n' cool, man," answered a jazz buff. "Yeh, right," said the hip-hopper.

The mist that had enshrouded the chickens began to slowly dissipate and the cool sounds of Monk, Miles, and The Bird began to fade, giving way to the pulsating rhythm of hip-hop that emanated from within the mist. For a few brief moments the two music mediums threw down! Gradually the cool sounds of Jazz faded into the background giving Rap its props on the stage of time. Its throbbing rhythm was now pumping full volume, as a d.j., suspended above the throngs of peopole, worked up a sweat. "What in hell kind of music is that?" said a Jazz lover. "It's funky fresh 'n' slammin' G," answered a hip-hoppa. "Sound like noise to me," said the jazz buff.

The mist that surrounded the rooster and hens began to fade, revealing first the hens, who were transformed into back-up singers and dancers, their skin a rich ebony hue. They were dancing and singing, "Da Sweetman iz comin' you better start runnin'." The mist completely dissipated, revealing a strapping, young Black man of Mandingo lineage, who was transformed from the rooster to DA RUZSTA DA RAPPER! He wears dark glassed and is dressed in black, Karl Kani, ghetto couture, hip-hop gear. "I'm ready to git bizy," he yelled to the crowd. "Put yo' hans in da air 'n' lemme hear you say yooo, yoooo. Check it out:

*Da Sweetman iz comin' gita runnin' 'n' da rappers be rhymin'*

# Aubu

If it ain't one thing sho-nuff is another
Wait a minute, looka here, lemme rap to ya brotha:
Back in da day de usta call me RUZSTA
Did'n' take no static did'n' take no slack
Ran my game on the downtown train runnin' on da uptown track
Cock-a-doodle-do da RUZSTA comin' through
Takin' care biz like da mailman
In da rain, in da snow, in da gloom a da nite. My momma prayed for me
Cause I won't livin' right
Back then I was Mack, Back then I was a con
I gave it all up somethin' better came along
Naw my head's in one place, yours in another
Wait a minute look a here
Lemme rap to ya brotha:
Ther's static in da 'hood 'n' da news ain't good
It's a down right pity whut goin' down in da city
Shoot em up in da school yard, children are 'fraid
Homeboy ain't gotta job but he wanna git paid
Times are hard 'n' street's gittin' meana
Everybody tryin' t' go somewhere where the grass is greener
It's wack!
Da way we'r living in fear
If I had some money I'd git up outa here
Da Sweetman iz comin' gita runnin' 'n' da rappers be rhymein'
If it an't one thing sho' nuff is another
Wait a minute looka here
Lemme rap to ya brotha:
Ya think ya got it goin' on black but ya nuttin' but a junkie
Lookin' funny 'n' smellin' all funky
Down on yo' knees 'n' ya know ya not prayin'
Don't play yo self, you know what I'm sayin'
You got static in yo' attic 'n' yo' brains erratic
My rap's emphatic I've said it befo'. Women ain't bitches 'n' de ain't no ho'
Da Sweetman's comin' gita runnin' 'n' da rappers be rhymin'
If it an't one thing sho' nuff is another
Wait a minute, looka here, lemme rap to you brotha
G you' like a B-ball bouncin'

12

*Shuckin' 'n' jivin' 'n' forty-ouncin'*
*In da springtime, summertime, winter time time movin' on fast, git up off yo' ass*
*Git yo' head together git to gittin' git a job*
*Workin for da butcher, for da baker or da candle stick maker*
*'Fo' you find yo' se'f takin' a ride wit da undataka*
*'N' yo' momma be cryin' 'n' feelin all weary as she follow da hearst to*
*da cemetery*
*If it an't one thing sho-nuff is another*
*Wait a minute, look a here, lemme rap to ya brotha*
*Life is what it is 'n' it ain't fair*
*Git to gittin no matter what*
*When da goin' git rough*
*You gotta be tough like a Timex take a lickin' 'n' keep on tickin'*
*'N' say a little prayer - Naw I lay me down to sleep, I pray to the lord my soul to keep*
*Yo' G I hope ya heard what I said*
*Thank ya for my daily bread—WORD!*

The crowd went wild and woof-woofed their approval. Mother Carye threw both arms up over her head as she turn around and around blowing kisses to the crowd. "Let me hear you say, 'The Sweetman is coming.' The crown joined in with enthusiasm. Then Mother Carye, Ruzsta the rapper, and the dancers disappeared into a cloud of haver and nosensification. And the rappers composed rhymes about what they saw.

# SILENCE

*W*arm spring days, blue skies, gentle rain, flowers. A warmth, a flame, an ecstasy fills my mind, heart, and soul when I contemplate the verities of this Awesome Universe. Creatures great! Creatures small! Thy hand, O Eternal Love, made them all. A baby is born and journeys through the seasons: Spring, summer, autumn, winter, the final season—THE END. The beginning. Silence. Vast, vast reaches of space, incalculable numbers of stars, planets, solar systems. Worlds! Worlds deep, deep in the cosmos. Everything in its place, governed by law!

My responsibility in this life is to study, investigate, contemplate, and meditate. In so doing, I grow closer to the Creator, which is the Law of all life. There is no language that is adequate to express it. Therefore it is extremely difficult for me to attempt to explain, verbalize, form into some sensible explanation the external vastness of it all. Therefore, I babble like a madman in the presence of it. So I contemplate, meditate, reflect, and understand inwardly the sweetness of love, complexity, and the simplicity of it all. SILENCE.

SILENCE! Ah, flowers in yonder meadows bloom. Oh, death upon me slowly creep, for yonder green forest is yet filled with a multiplicity of living things I have not yet looked upon. Mountains, oceans, seas, and crystal waters flowing in a thousand thousand gentle streams.

Dark clouds gather. Darker and darker they grow. Thunder! Lightning sets the heavens ablaze. Rain, rain, rain. The oceans and seas grow angry as crystal streams overflowing. Violent, destructive, tornado winds, angry! Whirling, funnel-shaped clouds destroying all in their narrow paths. Mountain tops and the floors of the oceans erupt, regurgitating fire—liquid fire—from their bowels. Nature rages angry, visiting destruction upon all that it has given birth to. The lamentations of man and beast go unheeded. The cry of infants are stilled…Summer, autumn, winter.…Warm spring days, blue skies, gentle rain, flowers.…Oh how great thou art! Oh sweet mystery of life! SILENCE.…

# DA SWEETMAN IZ COMIN'

**N**ight fell as soon as Mother Carye and her brood disappeared. Then a strange event occured. The sun rose in the east. The moon in the west. They passed each other seven times, then eclipsed. This having occurred, a strange calm prevailed over Harlem, mingling with the carnival-like atmosphere. Children who ran amuck earlier were sitting on the curb or on the shoulders of their parents like angelic cherubs. The young men who earlier had worn their jeans so low that their asses showed, pulled them up enough to cover that offending part. The anticipation was so intense you could cut it with a knife.

The moon and sun having passed each other for the seventh time, the sun returned to the east to make ready for its morning rise. The moon at its fullest, remained, casting its luminescence upon the waiting crowd, most of whom seemed becharmed. People were petting and embracing the vicious pit bulls as though they were kittens. The ladies who rushed from the beauty parlors when Mother Carye first arrived, dotted the crowd with their nails and hair in various states of undoneness creating a bizarre sight indeed.

The word of The Sweetman's coming had spread and the press corps from around the world had gathered by this time and were clawing, scratching, and knocking each other down, jockeying for a prime spot. The female news persons were particularly vicious, but Spike Lee and his 40 Acres 'N' A Mule Filmworks were cool and laid back, capturing this rare moment on film. Stay tuned for "Da Sweetmen Iz Comin'! The Movie."

A group of enraptured church ladies looked longingly up the street in the direction in which The Sweetman would appear. One of the ladies muttered as though in a trance, "I knew The Sweetman personally, from the good ol' days." "From what I gather, you *knew* him real well, I hear tell you use to *work* for him," said one of the other ladies. "Don't you start no shit. You can't throw no stones, 'cause you didn't wear your drawers tied tight, 'round you legs Missy. As a matter of fact, back then you didn't wear any. You would pile your naked ass right up on the bar stool 'tisin' men to buy you drinks," hissed the first lady. "Umph!" went the other ladies in the group in unison. "I hear tell that Sweetman is the father of Rosemary's baby," blurted a man standing nearby. "Hush yo' mouf 'n' go 'way from here. That Night Train got you talkin' fool talk," said one of the ladies. The man walked away mumbling to himself, as he took a swig from the bottle.

*21*

A little boy looked up at his mother and said, "Mommy, when is Tweetman comin?" "Soon," answered the mother. "Mommy, I want to be like Tweetman when I gro up." "No, I don't think so," the mother said. Da Sweetman Iz Comin, t-shirts appeared out of nowhere, and everyone was wearing one.

Greasy Pete the food vendor, having sold out of food, was pissed. Being a man of entrepreneurial insight, foresight, as well as greed, he was not about to be saddled with hindsight. Pete was enterprising, to say the least. "Where in the hell am I going to get a fresh supply of meat from at this time of night," Pete mused to himself. Looking around, Greasy Pete spotted a large pile of garbage. Quickly, Pete walked briskly over to the pile of refuge and gave it a vicious kick and a swarm of fat rats ran from beneath it with Pete in hot pursuit. Pete and the rats disappeared behind his food cart. There was a brief squeal and soon Pete stood up from behind the food cart smiling as he harked his sudden supply of shis-ke-bobs. "Git yo shish-ke-bobs here," bellowed Pete, as a horde of hungry customers knocked each other down in their mad scramble to get one of Pete's fresh cooked rat-ke-bobs.

Far as the eye could see, there was a sea of humanity awaiting the arrival of Sweetman. The Police on the beat became alarmed at the large number of Black people assembling and radioed police headquarters for reinforcements and the riot squad, the prevailing notion being, if more than two Black people gathered and said "hello" to each other, a conspiracy or insurrection was afoot. Squads of ghetto birds flew overhead with searchlights sweeping the rooftops for those Blacks of revolutionary bent. African drums throbbed in the distance. Lightning streaked across the sky. Thunder rolled in the heavens. A deep calm descended upon Harlem. The crowd fell silent.

Emerging out of the night, riding on an ass (or whatever), fanning himself with palm branches, Sweetman appears. "Here he comes," someone yelled. When Sweetman emerged into full view, all the children ran to greet him. The children's parents ran after them. "Come back here," they yelled. "Leave 'em be," commanded Sweetman. He spoke to the children saying: "Y'all come to The Sweetman. He loves you. Do you know why I' come back? Do you? Well, let me tell you. I Love You! In yo' faces the beauty I see. I'm a part of you 'n' you are a part of me. In yo' eyes I see the stars of heaven shine. Spring, summer, autumn, and winter are the seasons we all pass through. You are the mornin', I'm evenin'. You are spring, I'm autumn. You are the sunrise, I'm the sunset. Look! My young friends, the mountains, oceans, seas, birds, flowers, clouds, and angels. All beautiful things, I see them all in your eyes. If no one else loves me it matters not. You love me and that means a lot, Y'all com' on. Git up mule."

The children followed Sweetman down the street. Shouts of "welcome Sweetman," "What's up Sweets," "We love you Sweetman," came from the crowd as Sweetman and the children proceeded to the Apollo. The marquee lit up **HARLEM WELCOMES THE SWEETMAN!!!** "Whoa," says Sweetman to his ass. He dismounts, and says to the children, "Y'all be good now, go back to yo' mommas." To the parents he says, "Take these young 'on's on home. It's gittin' late 'n' I want to confabulate wit you ol' folk." Sweetman ties his weary horse to a parking meter. A young police officer, who was three feet shorter than a midget, waddles up to Sweetman and taps him on the leg with his night stick and says, "Boy, you can't tie your ass to this parking meter. It's not a hitching post, and it's against the law. So get your ass outta here and take your ass with you, or I'll place your ass under arrest." With eyes blazing and smoke coming from his nostrils, Sweetman whirls and looks up, then down. "Oh there you are. Let me tell you something officer, ah, ah," stutters Sweetman, bending over trying to see the officer's name tag. Sweetman reaches down, picks the officer up, looks at his name tag, puts him down and says, "Let me tell you something, Shorty Shortstuff, you little sawed off officer of the law. Don't ever call me boy or la' yo' han's on me, unless you are healin'." Officer Shorty Shortstuff backs up, looking as though he had seen the devil.

Sweetman walks out into the middle of the street, turns around, and looks up at the Apollo shaking his head. "It's good to be back," he says. What a sight he was, looking like three miles of rough road. Sweetman's habiliment is an old torn and tattered red suit that had seen better days. He and the suit had been through the mill more than once. The lapels are festooned with a withered white carnation, which he wears on the left, and on the right, an oversized white button with red letters that say "Ignorance kills!" To complete this quixotic get up, Sweetman wears a ragged pink shirt, dingy white string tie, and sports high-heeled platform shoes that superfly pimps wore in the '60's and '70's.

Sweetman is a study in contradiction. In spite of his apparent insolvency, he adorns his person with genuine gold rings, chains, and pendants. When queried about this "Looks can be deceiving," or "You can't judge a book by it's cover," is his response. In his right hand, Sweetman always carries a red silk hankerchief which he uses to mop his brow, or dab his lips when he's told or is about to tell a risque joke. A red stick decorated with the feathers that fall every seven years from Mother Carye's chickens' tails. Three black rabbits' feet and three neck bones of a wild boar, painted white. On his left arm, he carries his ever-present red Macy's shopping bag which contains his meager belongings: books that, he says, hold the secrets of life—roots, and magic dust.

On his head, Sweetman sports a long shaggy wig, which he pulls off at times for dramatic effect, sending his audience into convulsions of laughter as he stands with the wig in his hand, revealing a shaved head, except for two patches of hair on either side, which is straightened and moused to stand up like horns, making him look like the devil himself. With a bemused look on his face he rolls his eyes heavenward and licks his lips.

Sweets, as the hip-hoppas refer to Sweetman, says, "Sweets is illin', trippin', buggin', wack!" Older people say he's out to lunch, touched upstairs, not wrapped too tight, or that fool is crazy. Some years back in Chicago, a preacher said to Sweetman: "You are a bellicose ol' heathen who has mis-lived, and you are two biscuits short of a church picnic. Come and be saved!" Sweetman shot back "Kiss my ass!" In France, they say that he is *boleverse,* but some old timers around the country say that he is a haruspex, storyteller, harbinger of what's to come, reader of the times, who brings his message through the medium of lampoonery. In spite of his tomfoolery, Sweetman's mordacious, rhapsodical middlesquiddledge (?) and grandiloquence without a doubt will leave one in a state of hugger-mugger and has been known to make a dead man or woman laugh. This tale has circulated for decades: Down in Chitterlinswitch, a little town outside of Gittchiegummie, Georgia, a Miss Tillie Tyson (no kin to Mike) was being funeralized. Miss Patricia Pryor (no kin to Richard) had just finished a hymn and Pastor Preston Peterson was standing behind the pulpit (with his fly open) and had just began to preach when Sweetman showed up at the service with a bunch of withered wild weeds and flowers. Sweetman tiptoed up to Miss Tillie's casket and laid the flowers upon her chest, then bent over and whispered into Miss Tillie's ear. The tickling of the weeds on her chest and whatever it was that Sweetman whispered to her aroused Miss Tillie from her lugubrious slumber.

Looking up and seeing Sweetman standing over her bier, she sat up and waxed hysterical. Her laughter sent the mourners fleeing from the church, overturning pews and knocking each other down. In the melee, a woman left her child behind. "Miss, your baby is still in the church," someone said to the young mother. "Well, she will stay there, 'cause I ain't going back up in there to get her," the mother said. Paster Peterson stood frozen, clutching a prayer book, and muttered, "Oh shit, I mean...Oh Lord, is you punishing me for my sins? I won't mess with Miss Pryor no mo'!" If perchance, you should venture pass the cemetery where Miss Tillie reposes, you will hear laughter issuing forth from her grave.

Sweetman, having stood in the street looking up at the Apollo for a while, picked up his red bag and walked up to the locked door of the theater. He raised his *juju* stick and waved it across the doors three times and uttered: *ugamooga!!* The doors opened as though by an unseen hand. As he enters the theater, he looks back at the crowd and waves his hand, indicating they should follow him inside.

"Y'all com' on," Sweetman says, as he heads down the aisle of the Apollo like a king with his subjects following him. He marches up on the stage and enthrones himself upon a stool. I shall never forget that spectacle. What a sight!!! The house was jam-packed, reminiscent of by-gone days when great entertainers like James Brown, The Supremes, Sam Cooke, Otis Redding, Ruth Brown, and scores of others of like note packed and rocked this grand old house. Even now, I can sense their presence.

Perched up on that stool like royalty holding court, The Sweetman raised his *juju* stick, and the crowd responded with a thunderous standing ovation in deep appreciation of his return. Sweetman, basking in the piquancy of the moment, dethrones himself from the stool, his eyes changing from smoldering coals to twinkling pools of appreciation. He moved the stool to stage left, then walked back to center stage, picked up his ever-present red bag, and walked to the edge of the stage, sat the bag down, and raised his arms until they were paralleled, making his body resemble a human cross. Arching his head upward until he could see the last balcony, moving it from left to right, thus recognizing all in the house, bringing his head back to its normal position, he bowed, then let his arms fall slowly to his sides. The house fell silent.

Meanwhile outside on the street, thousands who could not get into the Apollo milled, as the police kept a wary eye under the able command of a sister, large and in charge...Captain Joyce Stephen, Deputy Commander of the 28th Precinct.

## Aubu

Deacon Freddy Bivens stood on the corner of African Square, at 125th Street and Adam Clayton Powell Jr. Boulevard, staring up at the Theresa Hotel, musing of days gone by. Back in the day this grand old establishment catered to the rich, the powerful, and the celebrated. It was once the residence of the late U.S. Secretary of Commerce, Ronald (Ron) Harmon Brown, and where young Charles Rangel, now a representative in the U.S. House of Representatives, worked as a desk clerk. The Theresa Hotel is now an office building, a shadow of it's former glory looking like a tired hooker slinging hash in a greasy spoon, too old to ply her trade. A sad reminder of the so-called 'good ol' days'. For a moment, I thought I heard Duke Ellington's "Take The A Train"...

Back in the theater, Sweetman grabbed a nearby mike. Everyone knew he was getting ready to git bizy!. The expression on his face had changed to one that said: Don't mess with me!!! He was ready to address the most discriminating and demanding audience on earth. He said, "Wut up Apollo?" "Wut it is Sweets," someone yells from the audience. "Everything is everything, ain't no never mind to me," Sweetman answered.

Of course, there's one in every audience: a heckler. "Why don't you git somebody to fix yo' suit, Sweetman?" someone said. "I would, but yo' Momma is too busy takin' care of my other needs," Sweetman shot back. The audience laughed, clapped, and woof-woofed their approval of Sweetman's come back as he stood smiling in the glare of the stage lights and flash bulbs. The crowd quieted down and Sweetman spoke:

# SWEETMAN SPEAKS

# The Early Years

*The ability to laugh at life is right at the top, with love and communication, in the hierarchy of our needs. Humor has much to do with pain; it exaggerates the anxieties and absurdities we feel, so that we gain distance and, through laughter, relief.*

Sara Davidson

*F*or all who don't know me, Sweetman is my name. Pimpin' us' ta be my game. Back in the day I hung out on the corner, profiled in my clothes, snorted coke up my nose, took money from da 'ho's, 'n' never worked a day in my life. The word 'work' irritated me.

You see, I always knew what I wanted to be. Why, I can remember when I was a little bitty boy, oh 'bout six years ol', da teacher she called on me in class one day, she said, "Little Sweetman, what do you want to be when you grow up? Come on, don't be shy!" "Pimp, I said," "WHAT!" Da teacher blurted. I never will forget the look that came 'cross her face. "You don't want to be nothing like that, child!" "Yessum, I do won' be pimp, 'cause pimp, he don' work 'n' he have lotta money, pretty clothes, 'n' he have a lotta ladies 'n' all dey names is 'ho', 'n' Miss 'ho', she git money from a man named John, 'n' iffin' Miss 'ho' don' give pimp nuff money, pimp he git mad 'n' put he foot up a alladator ass. Dat's how he gits alladator shoes on he feets."

After school, the teacher grabbed me by the han' 'n' took me home to my momma 'n' daddy. She said, "You all had better do something about this boy, and do it quick. The child wants to be a...a...a...Oh Lord, a pimp!" My momma said, "I kno' the chil' was crazy, but Lord I didn't kno' he was this crazy!"

My daddy gave me five cross my lips. Back in them days, ol' folks would whup yo' ass. Well anyway, my daddy said, "Don' worry 'bout it Miss Grumplerumpple (that was the teacher's name), we will take care of this situation." So my momma 'n' daddy took me down in the woods to see the *voodoo* woman. My daddy said to the *voodoo* woman, "This here boy wana be a pimp. Please work yo' *mojo* 'n' take' dat fool stuff outta his head." The *voodoo* woman said to my momma 'n' daddy, "leave this troublin' matter in my han's. I'm goin' run my *mojo* 'cross 'im three times 'n' put 'im to sleep. When he wake up, he will see de light 'n' all dat pimp fo'shness will be gone from his head." The *voodoo* woman closed her eyes 'n' she commenced to moan 'n' groan. Then she ran her *mojo* 'cross me three times 'n' said, "*Uggamogga*, go to sleep lil' Sweetman, now wake up 'n' tell us whut you see 'n' whut you go' be." I woke up feelin' groggy like. I rubbed my eyes, yawned, 'n' said, "I see 'ho's 'n' I go' be pimp." The *voodoo* woman scratched her head 'n' mumbled, "I mus' be loosin' my grip.

Dat will be a dollar suh." "For what?" my daddy said. "You can't work roots on a fruit fly, much less a six year old crazy boy. I ain't go' give you nothin'." The *voodoo* woman got mad. "Give me my money! Don' make me mad, 'cause I will mix up som' strong po'shun 'n' cause you to walk backwards mister," she screamed as we wus walkin' way. My daddy looked back 'n' said, "Woman, take yo' po' shuns 'n' roots 'n' stick 'em up." "Naw, naw," my momma said, cuttin my daddy off. "Com'on Sweetdaddy 'n' leave her be." "A'right Sweetmomma," daddy said.

When I was 'bout twelve years old, my daddy woke me up one mornin' to the sound of some dogwood switches. My daddy said, "Boy, git yo' ass out dat bed. I go' tak' you wit me to de cotton field t'day. Teach you how to work'n' be a man. You won' go to school, so you go' go to work." I took deathly ill. So my daddy put me in de wagon 'n' took me to da doctor. Da doctor 'xamined me. After he finished he said to my daddy, "This boy is allergic to something" My daddy said, "I kno' wut it is. It' call' 'work', 'n' iffin he don' hurry 'n' git over his allergy, or whatever the hell it is, I go' git rid of it for 'im." For the next couple a years, I worked in da cotton fields wit' my daddy 'n' I didn't like it one bit, but my better judgement prevailed upon me to keep my mouth shut.

Sweetman mops his brow and dabs his lips with his red handkerchief, and rolls his eyes. Anyone who has ever heard The Sweetman speak knows when he was about to tell a tall tale or stretch the truth: I can 'member this like it was yestiddy. You all know when you git 'roun' 'bout fourteen years old yo' hormones commence to exert themselves and you git frisky. Ha, ha, ha... Oh my goodness. I recall a neighbor gal, by the name of Sally Mae Sayer, who was sweet on me. Everytime she saw me she would com' a sniffin' 'roun' me like a she houn' in heat 'n' I'd prance like a bull 'roun' a heifer. She would eye the front of my britches, and my eyes had surveyed her ampledge more than once.

One day, I asked her momma if I cou'd com' a callin' on Sally. Mrs. Sara Sayer she said, "Yes," so Sally 'n' me we start sparkin' 'n' went straight to da woods 'n' she let me "have my way" wit' her. Today you young people call it "gittin down" or "gittin bizy."

Well, the next day her momma came a tearin' over to my house just a hollerin' 'n' carryin' on 'bout' she was goin' to kill me, cut my pecker off 'n' feed it to the birds. Well, let me tell you, the birds wou'd have had a beak full. They wou'd been perched up in the tree smil'n from ear to ear.

Anyway, my momma ran out the house, "What is all the commotion 'bout?" She asked! "It's yo' heathen son, Sweetman," bellowed Mrs. Sayer, who was steamed. "What did he do?" my momma asked. "Look at her," Mrs. Sayer said, pointing to Sally Mae. "You justa look at my precious, pure, innocent baby. Your hot assed boy don' gone 'n' plowed her ground. My chil' has been deflowered, her petals plucked, her leaves have fallen. She is ruin't. Look at her hair standin' all over her head. Her clothes all ever' which-a-way, her ninnies is sore, her bloomers tore 'n' I don't think she will pee anymore!" "If my boy did all that to her," said my momma, "why is she standin' here lookin' at my Sweetman grinnin' like a chess cat?"

Oh my goodness, I was a pistol in my time. One day Mrs. Gloria Goodstuff, who lived a couple of miles from us, said to her daughter Gail, "Honey go out 'n' milk the cow, and remember if a young man come pass the house while you're milkin' the cow, I want you to stop 'n' come in the house until he passes by, 'cause young boys 'n' men have ugly needs that a woman should never satisfy until she's married to him. Even then try to git 'roun' it. Say you got a headache. If you must do it, close your eyes, lay still 'n' don't move, only loose wanton woman throw their limbs into the air 'n' holler 'n' carry on like they is bein' kil't. Just do it 'n' pray it's soon over. Which it is most of the time. Honey some men are so hoggish they want to do it all night. Just hope you will not marry a man like that, who want it all the time, anytime, anywhere, anyplace, and with anybody. Umph, umph, umph, heaven help a woman who git saddled wit' a beast like that. If you do, he will have you havin' chullins like a cat havin' kittens. Most men, even if you give in to their doggish needs, they will still run off 'n' do it with loose women who posses those unwomanly skills, 'n' there's no tellin' what kind of sinful ailment he will bring home and give you. Why I even hear tell that some of these trollops even handle a man's...down yonder. So honey, when you git married remember, lay still 'n' do your wifely duty and don't utter a sound. Even if you like it, don't let on to him, 'cause if you do he will never leave you alone. Some men are so intemperate, they tell the woman what to say during these libertine sessions and often times when he nears the completion of these carnal carryin' on's, he will utter the most foul language, like the devil himself had gotten into him. So honey remember what momma jus' tol' you, naw go on 'n' milk the cow."

A few minutes passed, then Simple Sam passed by the house. Gail's momma called out the window, "Honey come in the house." Gail went into the house until Sam passed by, then she went back outside and continued milkin' the cow. A few minutes later Jim Hunglow came toward the house, and Gail went into the house until he passed. After Jim was out of sight, she went back to milkin' the cow. Then I came down the road toward' the house. Gail's momma looked out of the window and saw me. "Oh God, Sweetman is comin'! Hurry honey, come in the house and bring the cow!" Mrs. Goodstuff was the first woman in America to recognize the importance of sex education in the home.

The worst day of my life was while walkin' down a dusty road in Alabama, on a hot summer day in 1929. I was hotter than a fresh fox in a forest fire. Strollin' in my direction was a young white gal. Our eyes made connection. I said, "oooo weeee." "Will I ever," she said, "No, you will never," I said "Whar' there's life, thar's hope," she said. "Whar' thar's a tree, thar's a rope." I waxed rhapsodical 'n' started rappin' holes in her clothes 'n' rumors in her bloomers. We was gittin' down, I looked up, thar' stood her daddy, so we jump up. He started buggin' 'cause we was doin' mo' 'n' huggin'.

He said, "Boy, dang you, I go' hang you!" He was the Grand Dragon of the KKK, you see. He grabbed me, put me on a horse, a rope 'round' my neck, 'n' said, "Boy, no nigra is go' mess wit' a daughter of mine. I go' put bullets whar' the sun don't shine." I started rappin' 'n' rappn' fast; that was the only way I wus goin' to save my ass. I said, "Deeky deeky yo knees is squeaky. You mad 'cause me 'n' yo' daughter jus' got freaky. Looka here, looka thar', up, down 'n' all 'roun'—yo' momma!!" Well sir, that outburst caught the Grand Dragon by surprise. While he was lookin' up in the air, I was otta thar'. (That's the day rap was born.) I ran home like a crazy child. In my head I could hear Billy Holiday singin', *Strange fruit, blood on the leaves and blood at the roots. Black bodies swingin' in the Southern breeze. Strange fruit hanging from the poplar tree....*

The word spread like wild fire throughout Gittchegummie county—A nigra boy don' carnalized a white gal—so the Klu Klux Klan was comin' for me 'n' da sheriff was a lookin'. All the roads leadin' out of Gittchegummie was blocked. Blood hounds was on my trail, a howlin' and barkin', itchin' to sink their teeth into som' black ass, which they considered a delicacy and 'ferred it to dog food. The only avenue of escape was through Devil swamp, where alligators measured twenty feet long.

My daddy ran wit' me down to the swamp, slapped me up side my head, stuffed some money in my pocket and said, "Boy, you are the biggest fool I have ever witnessed in all my born days. Me 'n' yo' momma has tried to teach you right. You don' wan' to work, you stand up in the school house and 'nounce you gon' to be a pimp, naw you git hot in da ass 'n' hit on the daughter of the Grand Dragon of the Klu Klux Klan. Lord have mercy!!! What have I raised???"

We looked up the hill 'n' the Klan was gettin' closer, so my daddy said, "Boy, you are on your own. I have done all I can do. I ain't goin' to stand here 'n' let "em kill me too." So my daddy ran off through the woods 'n' left me standin' thar'. I hollered, "Daddy don't leave yo' lit' Sweetman," but he didn't look back and he didn't stop runnin'. The sheriff was closin' in on me, so I took off down through the swamp. A big alligator looked up 'n' said to the others, "What da hell wus dat?" Another gator said, "I don't kno' whut it was, but if all the food moved through here at that speed, we all will starve to death."

I hid in the woods 'til nightfall, got on the Greyhound bus, came here to New York City, got off at the Port Authority Bus Station on 42nd Street. I walked out of the station, sat my bags down, looked up 'n' said, "This is my kinda town," and looked down, and my bags were gone. I had always heard New York was fast. I weren't in town more than five minutes before I was robbed, rubbed, felt, and fenagled. Before I could catch my breath, a man walked up 'n' put his hand up between my legs. I said, "Mister, if you don't get the fukk-funk away from me, I'll call the police." He said, "I am the police." Damn! I was always fascinated by the fast life, but this was too fast! I said to myself, let me git the hell up outta here.

I walked up to a White man 'n' said, "Excuse me sir, can you tell me whar' all the colored folks be hangin?" "Hangin? Boy you must be from down south. We don't hang negros up here in New York. If you want to find your kind, walk up Eighth Avenue to Harlem," he said. "How will I kno' when I git to Harlem?" The White man said, "You'll know. Around 110th Street the complexion of things will begin to change. You will see a lot of Jazz joints, chicken shacks and rib houses."

I remember when I first came to New York, Harlem was vibrant, radiant, nurturing. People were polite, friendly, courteous, well-mannered, and respectful. The streets and sidewalks were clean. Trees lined the boulevards. Good restaurants and clubs were in every block. You had your pick of movie houses: The Harlem Opera House, the Alhambra (now the

Department of Motor Vehicles) and the Masons' Lodge, located on Seventh Avenue (Adam Clayton Powell, Jr. Boulevard) and 126th Street, The Lafayette, the Odeon, The Roosevelt, The Douglas, The Loews on Seventh Avenue, The Victoria, The Regent and the Sunset to name a few. You could get a meal at Father Devine's for ten cents if yo' ends was short. Double-decker buses ran up 'n' down Seventh Avenue, open air trolleys on Lenox (Malcolm X Boulevard) and Eighth (Fredrick Douglas Boulevard) Avenues, and the 145th Street, 135th Street and 116th Street crosstown trolleys. Remember the EL? I know you old-timers know what I'm talkin' 'bout. Do you remember strollin' down Seventh, Lenox, Bradhurst, Edgecombe, or St. Nicholas Avenues on Sunday or a warm spring day or hot summer evening doing what the hip-hoppers today call "chillin"? We dressed to the "nines" back in the day. Naw days everybody got their clothes hangin' off their asses!—

Glancing down from the stage, Sweetman abruptly halted his confabulatory and stared down at a group of young men seated in the front row with spikes of hair sticking up on partially shaved heads (looking like Coolio), boots untied and their Karl Kani jeans hanging low, super low between their legs with an attitude from hell. "What is this?" asked Sweetman. With his hands on his hips, continuing to stare at the young men, he said, "I kno' damn well that yo' Johnson ain't that long, that you have to wear yo' britches hangin' off yo' ass." Sweetman shook his head, "umph, umph, umph, what is this world comin to?" He continued.

—Look at yo' head. What did y'all do, go in the barber shop, sit in the chair 'n' tell the barber "Fuck up my head!" Umph!, I suppose you are wearing your boots untied so you can jump out of them quickly if the police are chasin' you. Ain't this a mess?—Sweetman was on a roll, the house was in an uproar with laughter. He continued.—Last week I hear tell out yonder in Watts, the police was chasin' a young boy 'n' he tripped 'n' fell, got all tangled up in his shoe strings. The police said, "Get up Hakeem you are under arrest." "How do you kno' my name?" Hakeem asked the officer. "It's carved on the back of your head," the policeman replied.

The young men stared up at Sweetman with a I-don't-believe-this-shit look on their faces. Sweetman made a crazy face, and the young men cracked up. One said, "Sweets is bugged." Sweetman continued with his rhapsodical middlesquiddle.

My first job in New York City was workin' in a 'ho' house, run by 'Big'

Bertha Brown. (Sweetman dabbed his lips with his red hankerchief). Big Bertha had two of the *biggest* diamond rings you ever saw in yo' life. Git yo' mind out the gutter folks! Back in those days, fancy 'ho' houses were called buffet flats. They had dining rooms where you could dine on the finest food 'n' drink in town. Big Bertha the madam, wore the latest fashions from Paris and her chef, "Big Dick" de Biggelo, served pig feet in an ambrosial champagne sauce, the house special, and bathtub gin flowed like water.

Upstairs thar' wer' numerous rooms that specialized in catering to the most jaded and lascivious appetites. Let's say that you desired to feast ruttishly upon a lady's "fur burger." There was a room for that. Or if perhaps you wanted to have yo' ass whipped to a fair-thee-well by Miss Tammy, the house dominatrix, you would go to the "whip room," whar the ass whupp'n business was so brisk, reservations had to be made a month in advance, because of the large number of White power brokers from downtown, who desired to be flogged into submission by Miss Tammy, a four-foot-ten Black woman, who wore a platinum blond wig 'n' cracked a mean whip. You could hear those men of high station yellin', "Spank me, Miss Tammy, I've been a bad boy." Miss Tammy would be tearin' their asses up. When she retired, she bought a mansion on bourgeois Sugar Hill in upper Harlem.

Man, those buffet flats were all over Harlem in the 1920's and 1930's. I see a lot of you old timers here tonight from way back then. You kno' whut The Sweetman is talkin' bout, so don't sit there 'n' act like you don' got sanctified, I'll pull yo' covers 'n' put yo' business in da street. Don't make me git raw.

The young hip hop men seated in the front row were paying rapt attention to Sweetman's every word. Well, well, wells, he continued, Anyway, those buffet flats catered to White people mostly, who flocked to Harlem in those days like flies to fermented fruit, to bourgeoisie Negroes, entertainers and such. Back then come night, thar' wer' so many White folks up here in Harlem, you would think that you were in Whitesville or on Park Avenue, but com' daylight Harlem turned black again, as the White men hurried back downtown, leavin' a trail of mixed Black babies behind. Of course naw, the White woman came too, especially them that was rich and bold, would venture up here frequently to Harlem to quill their Paphian appetite for dark meat at Big Bertha's, Eunice's, Minnie's or Mable's buffet flats, whar' those women of privilege would shed their jewels and furs like a snake sheddin' it's skin as they slid 'n' slithered out of their Houte Couture frocks from Paris and readied themselves to be mounted, or otherwise taken care of, by one of Mandingo lineage. As a matter of fact, The Sweetman provided many a cure for some of those ladies of wealth and leisure who were sufferin' from a' 'cute case of *jungle fever*. My nickname was "Service Station", cause I pumped so much gas. Some called me: "coffee", cause I grind so fine. Ha, ha, ha....Oh, my goodness, umph, umph, umph! Let me stop 'n' shut my mouf!

In those days I lived in the fast lane—express all the way. Kno' whut I'm sayin'? I was one chilly dude. I was so cool I walked sideways. I was lean, clean, 'n' mean. My hair was fried, dyed, 'n' laid to the side. I bopped down the street cool 'n' slo', rapped out the side of my mouth, 'n' talked mo' shit than a radio. When I sported a lid, the brim was broke ace, deuce, my lips, tres-four. My theme was "Let the good times roll!" I kept a pocket full of ends, but I was never satisfied. I wanted mo' 'n' I would git it, made me no never mind which ever way. The world was my oyster 'n' I was the pearl. Drank liquor from the top shelf, smoked reefer, snorted cocaine 'n' felt no pain. I was bad. I was so bad I could make a church woman sing out of tune, cause the organist to strike a sour note, 'n' make the minister come outa the closet 'n' scare a 'ho' in the right direction.

It was on the 'ho' stroll at the corner of 125th Street 'n' St. Nicholas Avenue, that's whar' I met Jamaica Slim. Jamaica was a big time pimp and he was also a pimpologist; he taught the art of pimpery. Jamaica drove a white Duzenberg, wore a white suit, white tie, white shirt, white hat with a big white feather, white shoes, 'n' his main lady was white. He had a pet alligator that he painted white, which he led 'roun' on a leash and would unleash it upon anyone who crossed, came too close, or rubbed him in the wrong direction. I suppose you could conclude that Jamaica Slim had a severe case of *white fever*. He was the meanest dude aroun'. He was so bad you needed an appointment to speak to him. If you made the mistake of doin' so without one, Jamaica would 'sic' the gator on you and make it take a nip out of your rear end, which was the gator's favorite snack.

It was Jamaica's custom to call all his ladies together on Friday evening and whup em. If he didn't, they wouldn't know that it was the weekend, 'cause he worked 'em so hard during the week, the days ran together on 'em. I admired Jamaica and wanted to be like him, so did the other young street players.

I got the nerve to walk up to him one day, and before I could git a word out my mouth, the damn gator was two feet from my ass. I said, "Jamaica, all I want is for you to teach me to be a bad ass dude like you." "Git your arse 'way from me mon, I te'ch you nottin'. You won' to be lik' me, go do yo' t'ing e'se wh'r' mon." Everybody on the block was laughin' at the way Jamaica had ranked me. I felt lower than shark droppin's, 'n' that's on the bottom of the sea. I plotted to git even. Nobody talk' to Sweetman like dat 'n' expect to slide.

I wanted what Jamaica had. He mus' had 'bout a hundred ladies workin' for him and I was determined to take 'em 'way from him. Plus I wanted to even the score for him comin' down on me in front of my boys. I made up my mind what I was goin' to do. Jamaica I'ma bus' yo' ass, I said to myself.

I ran my plan by my homeboy Foots. Foots' eyes bugged out of his head. He stuttered and backed away from me like I had somethin' catchin'. "Oh fuck!" he blurted and ran lik' a bat outta hell. I yelled, "Hey Foots, what's up man?" But he never stopped runnin'. He never looked back. Homes got in da wind.

I went 'n' copped som' blow from a dope dealer named Mr. Good Blow, who was known to blow mo' 'an coke. I got my head bad tore down like Cooter Brown. Understand whut I'm sayin'? Then I stopped in Leroy's, ordered two double shots of Johnny Walker Red, downed it, went to my crib, and picked up rosco, grabbed a hand full of wolf tickets and headed back to the 'ho' stroll. Jamaica Slim was parked around the corner from the stroll in front of the Baby Grand Night Club, leanin' up against his Duzenburg chillin' 'n' rappin' to his main squeeze 'n' da gator suckin' on a mango. With the alcohol and cocaine, I was feelin' no pain. I walked right up in Jamaica's face. People started runnin' for cover. "Are you crazy mon," he said. "Yeh, I'm crazier than a muthafuker, Naw shut the fukup. I got a handful of wolf tickets 'n' you're buyin' all of 'em," I said. He saw that I meant business so he started to unleash the gator.

More people started to run for cover. "Are you crazy mon?" Jamaica said. I didn't answer. He saw that I was gettin' closer to him so he started givin' the gator slack on it's leash. "D'n't y'u com' no clos'r mon, I mak' me gator bit you up yo'r fukin' arse," said Jamaican. "Screw you and yo' scaley-ass gator," I said. He turned the gator loose and it was inchin' closer. I pulled out my heater and shot it. "Woff ticket number one," I said. Then

# *Aubu*

I slapped the mango out of Jamaica's hand, stuck my equalizer in his face 'n' said "I'm da man! Woff ticket number two. And another thing, I's from alligator country. As a matter of fact I outran a herd of them suckers and thar's no such shit as a white alligator. You got *white fever* so bad you went 'n' painted that poor 'gator' white. You should be charged with cruelty to animals. Naw, I'm going to tak' all of yo' 'ho's. Everything, 'cept them funny vines you wear. Woff ticket number three." Then I kicked Jamaica in his ass! Woff ticket number four. Made him skin the alligator and make me a pair of 'gators' right thar' in broad daylight. Woff ticket number five. After sellin' him the hand full of tickets, I ran him out of Harlem as Ray Charles was singing, *Hit The Road Jack 'n' Don't Come Back No Mo'*. In the streets only the baddest survive and eventually they get their asses kicked! But, what goes around comes around, sho' nuff—

On that note, Sweetman gave the young gagsta brothers in the audience a knowing stare, his tone of voice softened, his eyes bespoke understanding, and then, addressing the older people present, he said: "We reap what we sow," so says the scriptures. The sins of the fathers are visited upon the children. It's the law of cause and effect, no mo', no less! So stop blamin' the children for the world's problems, when we ol' folks kno' we are to blame. Moms Mabley told you that years ago. You done forgot so I'm tellin' you again.

Well, well, I see a lot of preachers in the house tonight. How you doin' Al? Oh my goodness, Reverend Al, I hear you'r runnin for Mayor of New York City. Naw com' on brother Al, walk maybe, but you kno' you' is too big to run. More than one chicken has crossed your plate.

Sweetman mopped his face and dabbed his lips with that red handkerchief. Everyone knew by now that he was about to tell one of his jokes. Sweetman continues: "I'm reminded of this story everytime I see a preacher: One Sunday morning, Big Rev. and Little Rev. were sittin' in the pulpit waitin' for the service to start, 'n' pretty sisters wer' comin' into the church. Big Rev. said to Little Rev., "Little Rev., I bet you today's collection that I have 'bedded' mo' of these women in this church than you have." Litte Rev. said, "Naw I don't kno' 'bout that Big Rev. I don' had my share." Big Rev. said, "You skinny little sawed off half-assed preachin' fool, what you kno' 'bout a woman? Tell you what we goin' to do: every woman that comes through the church do' that you have saddled, say 'umph!'" A lady came down the aisle, Big Rev. went, "umph!" Another one came down the aisle, Litte Rev. went, "umph!" They both were goin' umph, umph, umph! Well it was almost time for the service to start and they were neck 'n' neck. Big Rev. looked at his watch and said to himself, "Thar's only five minutes left 'fo' the service start. It will look bad if this sawed off little, no preachin, son-of-a-gun have saddled mo' women than me, when I'm the head honcho of this church." At that moment, Big Rev's wife, daughter, and son came through the church do'. Naw, Big Rev. was married 'n' Little Rev. was single, so that would make Big Rev. have one up on Little Rev. A broad smile came across Big Rev's face, he reared back in his chair and went, "umph!" Little Rev. went, "Umph, umph, umph!"

The audience erupted! The crowd was in hysterics. Some fell to the floor, and rolled down the aisles as they woof-woofed and howled with laughter. Sweetman, with an impish smile on his face, stood with his hands on his hips, knowing that he had killed with that joke, which he says is about one hundred years old. Many in the audience hurried to the bathroom to pee.

I kno' how to mak'em piss on themselves, said Sweetman as he strutted stage right—All right you'll com' on, com' on git up! After the audience composed themselves, Sweetman continued: Well sir, gettin' back to Jamaica, after I chased him back to Kingston, I went and bought me a bad pair o'red wheels and a red silk suit to match. As a matter of fact this is what's left of it. Well, easy come, easy go. That's the way the ball bounces and the cookie crumbles.

After all what jumped off with Jamaica Slim, it left me hungry as a boar hog that han't been slopped in a month of Sundays. I hopped into my pimpmobile and cruised over to the whale station, The Fried Fish Factory, which was owned by Freaki Freddi 'n' his boyfriend Frank Frazier from Philly, to cop a grease. I'm laid back conversatin' wit' Freddy Bivens, a boot-legger out of Jacksonville greasin' on greasy fried flounder 'n' fries, when my main man Fly Floyd, also from Florida, flew through the do'. Hom' boy was trippin. "Sweets! Man what kinds shit you don' gon' 'n' don'? What kinda shit is you smoking? What is you sniffin' homes? Nigga, i-s y-o-u d-o-n' g-o-n' c-r-a-z-z-z-z-zy or wut? I heard you went 'n' fugged up Jamaica! You keep this shit up Sweets, som'body is go' bus-a-cap in yo' black ass," said Fly Floyd. I said, "Fly, don' sweat it. Ev'rything is ev'rything. I was just tellin' Bevins that I'm goin' after Ice Berg Slim next." Fly Floyd's eyeballs flew outta his head. He blurted, "Oh shit, I'm gittin' up in de wind 'n' far de fu'k up 'n' 'way from you. Sweetman, you git a man kilt!" I said, "My man, iffin that's be the way you be seein' shit, bye!" Freddy Bevins just shook his head.

I paid my bill and was on my way out the do' when Freaki Freddi flounced over to me and said, "When you goin' to give me some of that big black sweet thing of yours, Sweetman?" "When palm trees grow in Harlem," I said. Don't you'll kno' when I woke up the next day, palm trees were growing all over Harlem. Be careful what you say outta yo' mouf, you may have to back it up. From that day to this, Freaki Freddi has not stopped smilin' 'n' lickin' his lips.

By now I was 'bout twenty-one and the biggest pimp in Harlem. I was even bigger than Ice Berg Slim. Later that year I was invited to Chicago to attend the annual Pimps Convention, whar' I was awarded the annual Golden Pimp Award. I was the youngest pimp ever to have this (dis)honor bestowed upon him. I came back to New York 'n' showed my ass. New York was a' orchard 'n' I was the only apple in it. I lived 'n' lived fast. I ran with the cool, slick, down, hip, fast dudes 'n' dudettes. Hung out in clubs like Freddy Bevin's King-Kong Kingdom, drinkin' corn liquor, The Braddock, Small's Paradise, The Cotton Club, Connie's Inn, The Famous Door, whar' stars like Louis Armstrong, King Oliver's Creole Jazz Band, Bix Beiderbecke, Eubie Blake, Billie Holiday, Duke Ellington and many other great muscians and singers performed. The list is too long to mention all of them but most, if not all, have passed through this great house at one time or another—The Apollo!

Memories, memories. Oh Lord! I can hear Bessie Smith, who graced this stage mo' times than I can remember. I can hear her singing now: Down hearted Blues—"I've Got the World in a Jug; the Stopper in My Hand," or, "Bring Me a Pig Foot 'n' Another Bottle of Beer." Or, Ida Cox singing "Lawdy, Lawdy Blues", or Billie Holiday singin' "Gloomy Sunday", Minton's Playhouse...The Sa...". Sweetman lapses into a reflective state—quickly he snaps out of it—"Umph, umph, umph," he continues. The dance craze in 1936 was the truck 'n' could truck my ass off. I used to take a couple dozen of my ladies to the "Home of Happy Feet" as the Savoy Ballroom was called backed then. We would all be dressed in red. When me 'n' my ladies stepped through the do', the dance floor cleared. "Sweetman is here," somone would yell. Those were the good ol' days.

Yes! I had it all. Had mo' money than the law allowed. I dressed sharp, would talk loud 'n' 'draw' crowd. When I strolled into a juice joint I would yell out, "Have no fear, Sweetman is here. Run the bar, give everybody what they' drinkin' 'n' give me the bill." By this time, I had 'bout a hun'erd 'ho's on the stroll. I was making so much money, I had to hire a' 'ssistant pimp to check my traps. I was wheelin' 'n' dealin', cheatin' 'n' stealin', dealin' from the bottom of the deck, thar's a function at the junction—it's partytime, sho-nuff sho-nuff. I was a high roller on a roll as the years rolled by.

In the 60's, there were juice joints like Wellsworth, which was located at 126th Street 'n' Seventh Avenue, The Baby Grand, the home of Nipsy Russel for many years and the Palm Cafe, both of which was on the main drag, 125th Street. On Sugar Hill, the 400 Club, Lundy's, The Red Rooster and The Pink Angel was where I hung with dudes 'n' dudettes, pimps 'n' players. I hung-out, strung-out with my hized fuzuked uzup ozon smizoke, wizine, kizoke 'n' dizope. Wizine, wizimen 'n' sizong wisuz mizy thizang, doozo yuzu uzunda stizand wizut I zam sazayin'?

# THE DOWNFALL

**N**aw, my downfall came when I was invited by Richard, big time comedian out thar' in L.A., Richard Pryor. I hadn't seen Richard for some time, but I got a call from him one day back in the early 80's. He said, "Sweetman, com' on out here to L.A. man, I'm out here free-basin." I said, "What you doin' naw man, playin' the base fiddle free?" He said, "No, this is a new way to use cocaine." So I jumped on a plane 'n' hurried to L.A., sniffin' coke all the way.

The plane landed in L.A., I got out, hopped in a limo, the limo pulled up to Richard's crib, I got out, rushed up to the door 'n' rang the bell—ding-a-ling, ding-a-ling, ding-a—the door flew open and a big ball of fire went pass me. I jumped back 'n' said, "Damn, Richard! That shit mus' be good to set yo' ass a fire. Com' back here 'n' give me som'. Richard! Richard! Richard! Don't be selfish brother." But he never stopped runnin'. Seem' lik' he didn't hear me. I found out the hard way, when yo' ass is on fire, you ain't goin' to stop for a glass of ice water.

I jumped back in the limo. Hopped back on the plane 'n' hurried back to New York, cause I heard tell thar was a drive-in 'base' house on 145th Street 'n' Seventh Avenue. I drove my short up into the 'base' house, hopped out, unzipped my pants, dropped my drawers, 'n' tol' the baseman to base me all over! All of a sudden, thar' was a big explosion!!! I hauled ass outta da joint, wit mah ass on fire. A skeleton ran up to me 'n' said, "Yo mister, you got a light?" I said, "Git the hell away from me wit' yo' crack smokin' ass!"

Then I spotted a ice truck, so I took out after it, but I was cut off by a passel of snaggle-toothed children, who surrounded me tryin' to roast their hot dogs 'n' marshmallows. I howled 'n' hollered like a hurtin' hound from hell, "Git the fruit loops 'n' mother goose, what's the use away from me!" I screamed at the children. They ran like they had seen old Beelzebub. Except one skinny little gal, no mo' than six or seven years old. She put her hands on her boney hips and said, "Mister, you are a mean old selfish man. The Lord ain't goin' to bless you. I hope you will never find water to put yo' fire out. It wouldn' be burnin' if you wa'n' up in dat crack house—(out of the mouths of babes). —Naw, can I please roast my hot dogs?" "Hell no!" I screamed,......alhaaamuf......what ever that is. "I'm goin' to tell my momma you cussed at me," she said as she ran off. "Missy, for a skinny little gal, you got mo' mouth than 'Jaws'. You probably took after yo' yak,

yak, yakkn' moma," I yelled after her as she disappeared from sight. I said to myself: Why am I standin' here in the street wit mah ass afire, hollerin' at a child. I felt the heat, so I took off runnin' down Seventh Avenue, with mah ass in full flame, resemblin' the fires of hell! Hollerin' like a distracted man. A song that was recorded by Frankie Lane in the 50's started playin' in my head as the fire enshrouded my ass like Dracula's cloak: *The days are long, the nights are cool, each star is a shining pool of water, cool, cool, clear water....*

Sweetman pauses, he is sweating profusely, as though he was reliving his fiery ordeal. He reaches into his bag and takes out the palm leaves and fans himself, then mops his brow with his red handkerchief. "Whew, oh Lord!" Shaking his head from side to side, he continues: Well—well, well, well, I hauled ass down the street tryin' to find water, any kind of water.

I'm runnin' like a bat outta hell, looking for water. I spotted a man pissin' on the street. I hauled ass in his direction, hollerin' "Thar's water." I ran towards him yellin' "Give it to me." "I don't play that shit," the man said with a shocked look on his face. I grabbed a hold of his instrument of relief, so as to direct the stream of piss on the flames. "Please brother man," I said, "Let me have it!!! Piss on me 'n' put out this awful conflagration." The man pulled away from me and ran as though he had seen Freddy Krueger, with his thing hanging out. "Lord forgive me, I will never pee on the street in front of woman and children again," I heard him say as he disappeared from sight; leavin' me on my knees beggin' to be pissed on, on Seventh Avenue in Harlem, in broad daylight. I jumped up off of my knees. Took off in search of water. I spotted a little boy drinkin' a soda. He saw me comin' 'n' sensed what time it was 'n' ran for his life.

I continued runnin' like a bat outta hell down the Seventh Avenue. Out of the corner of my eye, the one that was not covered with fire, I spotted a pit bull in a' 'bandon buildin' nursin' her vicious offspring. I ran in the buildin' 'n' put the fear of gawd into the dog. Wrenched her titties from the puppies' mouths, threw them here 'n' yonder, 'n' fell on my knees (again) 'n' commenced to quill my thirst. That dog was so filled with fear her viciousness left her, 'n'she stood thar' 'n' let herself be milked as she entered into a state of canine hugger-mugger. "Hey man come here, look! A flamin'-ass bum is suckin' a dog's titties," A man yelled to another. The other man peeped through a hole in the wall of the 'bandon buildin'. His hair shot up on top of his head. He exclaimed, "Only in America!" Don

King's hair is still standin' up to this day. After I sucked the pit bull's titties dry, I ran like a bat outta hell, tryin' to find anything liquid or resemblin' water. James Brown was standin' on the corner, saw me runnin' towards him. He jumped back 'n' said, "Umph, good gawd, git back, looka here...."

In the middle of the block, thar' was a little Pentecostal Church and they were having service and the choir was singin', "Oh my Lord didn't it rain." When yo' ass is on fire, you will run in the direction of water. So I ran in the direction of the church, but when I got to the church do' the choir stopped singin' 'n' the preacher commenced to preach. He said, "Behold the end is near. We shall kno' when the end is near 'cause the spirit will descend from heaven on a chariot of fire." So I ran down the aisle of the church, out across the pulpit. The preacher's robe went up in flames. He jumped back and said, "Holy smoke, ain't this a bitch. I didn't kno' that the spirit was comin' this quick!" Fire will make a preacher cuss! I ran out the back do' of the church and jumped into the Harlem River to cool mah ass off, Umph, umph, umph.

Sweetman waxed preachy. Lord, Lord, Lord, you kno' I ain't had nothin' but pain and trouble," he said (lookin' heavenward). He ran back and forth across the stage waving his red his red handkerchief as though he was tryin' to put out a fire that still burned.

**U G L Y!!!**

*I* don't have no good luck. If lady luck offered me some, bad luck would beat me to it. Earlier today I stopped in a greasy spoon for a doughnut and a cup of coffee. The man behind the counter brought me my doughnut and coffee. He had his thumb in my coffee. I said, "Mister, why do you have yo' thumb in my coffee?" He said, "I'm sorry sir, I, I sprained my thumb and the doctor told me to keep it in something hot."

I said, "That's unsanitary!" He said, "If you think this is unsanitary sir, you should see how we put the holes in the doughnuts." I jumped up off of the stool to get the hellup out of that place, when a funny lookin' man, with his hair standin' all over his head 'n' his eyes painted purple, sitting a couple of stools away said, "Excuse me sir, if you're not going to eat that doughnut may I have it?" I said, "No! I'm not goin' to eat it. You are welcome to it, but didn't you hear the counterman say how they put the holes in the doughnuts?" "Yes I heard him. That's why I want it and I'm goin' to order another dozen to take home," he added, grinning from ear to ear. Umph! Ain't that a mess? Some people will eat anything. This is a crazy world.

Last week a judge slapped a' injunction on me, that prevents me from comin' within a thousand feet of a graveyard or a' undertaker's parlor, caus' he said I was so ugly. I'd make a dead man laugh. The judge said, "If I had the authority, I would give you life plus thirty days. Do you have anything to say before I throw your ugly ass out of my courtoom?" I walked up to the bench, pointed my finger in his face, 'n' said, "You, you old Judge Wopner lookin', black robe wearin', moth—." "Watch it, you are skating on thin ice," the judge said. I said, "Your Lordship, I mean your honor, I'm insects." "Incensed," the judge corrected. "Whatever," I shot back. "You have the temerity to call me ugly? I can talk 'bout ugly all night long. Starting with yo' ugly ass family. Yo' daddy look Freddy Kruger. Yo' momma is so ugly she can scare a pit bull off a meat truck. Yo' whole family is ugly. Halloween is their holiday. Don't git me started! Cause I can talk about ugly all night long!"

For instance: Last week I read in the newspaper, whar' the police confiscitated three hundred thousand dollars worth of drugs. They took it to the police station and locked it up in the property room. Next mornin' it was all gone. No one knows whar it is. I can tell 'em whar it is, just look aroun' the station house 'n' see who's nodin' 'n' scratchin', who didn't show up for work, who's driving a new Ferrarri 'n' who has left town. UGLY!!! Everybody is goin' crazy these days. Officers of the United States Navy took leave of their senses at that Tail Gate—No, Tail Hook—Convention 'n' gripped, grabbed, groped 'n' grinded with women against their will and otherwise showed their asses. The New York City Police Brass is still smartin' under the collar over that nude Police Convention that took place in the Nation's Capital, whar, some upholders of the law pulled their drawers off 'n' exposed their hidden parts. Upon returning to New York City, they came down with amnesia and hollered, "I don't remember."

That's ugly! I can talk 'bout ugly all night long. Sometime ago a police sergeant was caught walkin' his beat in Grand Central Station, wearing nothing but his pistol. He came upon a robbery in progress. The naked seargeant pulled his gun (the wrong one) 'n' yelled to the perpertrator, "Halt, or I will shoot!" The perpertrator bent over and said, "Go ahead honey, shoot mother." The other day I saw a one-armed pimp, chasin' a one-legged 'ho' in a wheel chair. Things are sho-nuff bad these days. I saw a family of midgets sleepin' in a mailbox. A hooker carryin' a sign that read: DISCOUNT! I can talk abot ugly all night long.

Naw you tell me if this ain't four or five bitches at the river with their drawers down. I kno' it make mine bunch up betwixt my legs, cuttin' off the circulation of my understanding, sendin' shivers up my 'way up yonder', when I see men of the cloth with self-righteousness cry out, "I have been called." They should be flogged when they fool, flim-flam, 'n' fleece their flock as they empty the church till. Some of these princely, priggish, postulatin', packer-slingin' priest 'n' preachers prance behind the pulpit like pompous peacocks, extolin' their parishioners to, "bridle your lust, come to the lord and repent, grid your loins against sin, blah,…blah…blah…," leavin' the church members in a state of pathos, while their own profligacy runs amuck like a herd of hot musk oxen, as their Fruit of the Looms are flung in one direction and their vestments in the other. Some have sunk so low they smoke crack and entwine themselves in the loins of the church secretary or with hookers, and in sadder instances, they help themselves to the little lambs of the fold!!

When caught, they weep 'n' wail like bitches in a briar patch, wax pusillanimous, and beg for instant forgiveness. "Lord, the devil has tempted your servant; my spirit was willing, but my flesh was weak," they moan. If their flesh is so weak, why didn't they go into a different line of work? Oh!

# DA SWEETMAN IZ COMIN'

I forgot, they were "called"! If this is what God is callin', can you imagine what the devil is conjurin' up? I kno' I don't want to see it! Ugly, ugly mess all over the world. Umph! I can talk 'bout ugly all night long. Naw you can began to see where da rappers get their rhymes.

Do you remember back som'time ago, when Rev. Jim Bakker fleeced his flock to live in palatial splendor, keeping Tammy in make-up, and their dog in a' air conditioned doghouse, and paid Jessica Hahn, the church secretary, a quarter of a million dollares of church funds to keep her mouth shut after he carnalized her? I'm told he turned her every way but loose. "This (the money) is a little something for helpin' me do God's work. I'm the shepherd and you are the sheep, that's why I grazed your grass," he said to her after helpin' himself to her womanhood. No sooner had Rev. Jim crawled from betwixt Jessica's quarters, that crazy gal ran straight to Playboy 'n' spread out her naked ass to the world and made enough money to buy herself a pair of state-of-the-art titties. Al Bundy calls them hooters. Anyway, when that matter was brought to Tammy Bakker's attention, she had a coniption. Overwrought, she went into her boudoir, fluffed her bouffant, applied an extra layer of makeup, and stuck two more eyelashes on her eyes that looked as though pregnant waterbugs had habitated her face. Jim Bakker went to jail. Tammy left Jim 'n' hitched up with his best freind, who is goin' broke tryin' to keep her in makeup. With the money Jessica got from Rev Jim, Playboy, and her 900 number, talk shows, and other lucrative deals, she became rich. Dirt sells!

Ugly—I can talk 'bout ugly all night long.

Who can forget that other holier-than-thou, evangelical, brimstone 'n' fire preaching preacher, Jimmy Swaggart, who yaked his fool hypocritical head off all the while he was chasin' hookers and engagin' in the most ruddish activities? When he got caught, he bellowed like a bull. "Oh Lord, I have sinned," he yelped. I believe he's still preachin'; I don't think too many people are listening. Then maybe they are. Many folks now days will listen to anything or anyone who lets the word 'God' slip from betwixt their lips.

Rev. Oral Roberts (you remember him?) took leave of his senses and in a state of holy hugger-mugger said that God was goin' to kill him if he didn't raise millions of dollars. Do you remember that? Seems to me, he could have sold that million dollar house he was livin' in—'least he would have had part of it. Then he said he could raise the dead. If he could raise

53

the dead, why couldn't he raise the money? Instead of beggin' 'n' buggin' poor folks for it? I don't understand no shit like this, ugly....These crazy preachers talkin' 'bout they are doing God's work. If what they are doin' is God's work, I damned well don't want to see the devil's work. That would be a bitch. I'll talk 'bout ugly all night long.

These days every time you turn around celebrities and persons in high places are bein' caught with their drawers down, hand in the till, their mouth or fly open and thar's no tellin' what will fly out. When caught these public icons bleet and bellow, "I'm sorry, I don't know what got into me" or "The devil made me do it." Some of the mess that's goin' on naw days the devil has not heard of.

What galls me is, no sooner than these crooks are caught, they go on the talk shows (which have sprung up like fungi) and make millions of dollars talkin' about their dirty deeds.

Ugly sells. Dirt sells. Case in point: You remember Boesky and Michael Milken, who milked Wall Street faster than Mike Mitchell of Mitchian milked his milk cow Milly. While they were wil'in away their time in those fancy country club prisons, the money that they had pilfered, syphoned, embezzled or stolen—(take your pick)—was stashed off shore somewhere accruing interest at such an alarmin' rate, it could be heard growing in the dark, makin' those *chevalier d'industries* richer, coupled that with what they make off of their book deals, t.v. appearances, movies and the fat fees they make on the lecture circuit—you get the picture 'n' da rappers keep on rhymein'...

I kno' you remember the *fille de joie* (ho), the so called Mayflower madam, and Joey Buttafuoco, the rapacious husband of Mary Jo, who laid a heavy hammer upon under-aged Amy Fisher, driving her to exact fire-power upon his wife, causin' her to talk out the side of her mouth. Amy was sent to jail. Snakeskin cowboy boot wearin' Joey spent a short time in the slammer. When released, the dirt crazed press laid out the red carpet for him. This wool-gatherer was ferried to and from jail in a limo, elevated to celebrity status, and inundated with book, movie, video as well as t v. deals. In short, he fucked his way to fame and fortune. Lust driven, this *pussy-crazedrascal* violated his probation by cruisin' the 'ho' stroll on Sunset Boulevard. He was sent back to jail. Released. Last I heard tell he was out in Californian makin' a movie!!! UGLY, I can talk about ugly all night long.

This case made world wide headlines: A well known English actor, horny Hugh Grant, tired of the delicate fragrance of Estee Lauder, came down with an acute case of *jungle fever* and desired to quill his ill, regulated passion with a *dememondaine* of ebony hue, a Ms. Devine Brown, a regular hooker, who frequented Sexset—oops, I mean Sunset Boulevard. That's a busy street. Well anyway, no sooner than Devine the trollop disengaged her lips from Hugh the trollopmongers quarter's, the editor of a British muckloid was in such a hurry to be the first to harvest this latest crop of American dirt (like the British don't have enough of their own), he could not wait for the Concorde, it was too slow he reckoned, it would be faster on foot, so he hauled ass across the ocean walkin' the water like—oh well, causin' the fish to lement, "Ain't this a wet bitch, man won't let nothing or no one have peace. Shit sail on the water, they throw all kinds of crap in the water, spill oil in the water, naw some damned fool is running on the water, what the fishfuks next?" The muckloid editor, upon reachin' these shores, hauled ass down Sexset—here I go again—Sunset Boulevard with $150,000.00 gripped in his hand, lookin' for hooker Devine. Upon locating her, he stuffed the $150,000.00 in her bra. "What do you want me to do?" she cooed. "Not a damn thing, I don t have time for that shit you're talking about! Tell me, what did you and horny Hugh do?", enquired the editor. "There's not much to tell. He wanted to git down, I went down, the cops came, I raised up, Hugh zipped up, we both were briefly locked up—that's it," said Devine.

The English muckmonger hauled ass back across the ocean, to get back to sexy old—I mean merry ol'—England before tea time and make his deadline. In the meantime, here in the good old U.S. of A., horny Hugh was a sensation, as he made the talk show rounds sayin', "I'm sorry," as scores of women took leave of their fackilations (ha ha), screamed and fainted at the sight of him, lustin' to do to Hugh free what Madam Devine did 'n' got paid $150,000.00 for doin'. She went on to become a world celebrity.

The editor of the British muckloid got paid well, as his tabloid was snapped up like flapjacks by English readers who are titilated by American dirt—goodness knows dirt lovers here in America have been well satiated with English muck 'n' mire, regarding the Royal dirty doin's in the House of Windsor—and horny Hugh cried, "I'm sorry," all the way to the bank. I can talk about ugly all night long. Dirt sells, so why in hell are some people squawkin' about gangsta rappers for? I don't understand mess like this. Gangsta rappers did not invent dirt, hypocrisy, double standards, lies, deceit and violence. The world as we knew it is built upon this muck 'n' da rappers keep on rhymein'.

I, The Sweetman, say unto you, what goes 'roun', comes 'roun'. What's good for the goose is good for the gander. I'll tal'—." The audience leaps to it's feet. The house is in an uproar as the crowd thunders its approval of Sweetman's grandiloquence. As cries of "Tell it like it tiz, Sweetman," filled the house, Sweetman appeared to be slightly annoyed that the audience had cut him off. He waves his red handkerchief across the room and once more silence prevailed, as Sweetman continued: I'll talk about ugly all night long.

Not long ago it was brought to my attention that a school teacher, Miss Belinda Browning of Bruster, was sittin' at her desk with her limbs agape, upon which gazed a twelve year old boy named Butch, his eyes glued 'n' glazed at the sight of his teacher's quarters. Miss Browning looked up; her face flushed; she blushed at seein' Butch's britches bulgin'; her bosoms took on a life of their own as she witnessed Butch's entrance into the pubescent phase of life. Butch, seeing Miss Browning's bosoms bulgin', began to bug and Miss Browning took leave of her faculties and ran away with the boy after school. They were caught in a motel, whar' Miss Browning, the teacher, was teachin' little Butch, who didn't weigh but a hundred pounds soak 'n' wet, the lickerish arts.

Detective Bill Billings, who busted Butch 'n' Belinda in the Blazing Blanket Motel, bugged, then broke into laughter when he witnessed Belinda with her limbs thrown asunder, with skinny Butch sandwiched betwixt her quarters, his narrow ass assaultin' the wind as Belinda flung her womanhood upon him, screamin' like a crazy woman, being consumed by the demons of carnality, and Butch lookin' like he had lost his mind. Umph! Ugly!

Miss Browning was arrested, fired from her teachin' position, and is out on bail awaitin' her day in court whar' she is expected to be sent up the river without her little boyfriend Butch. In the meantime. Miss Browning, Butch, and his momma Barbara appeared on Geraldo, whar' Miss Browning, holdin' Butch's skinny hand, explained to the world how much she is in love with the child and wants to marry him and raise a family. Geraldo asked Butch's momma, Barbara, how she felt about this troublin' situation. She broke down 'n' wept. "I'm so confused," she cried, then leaning over Butch she shrieked at Miss Browning, "You ol' 'ho'! You slut! You dirty bitch! You are older than I am, you will never marry my baby!" "How do you feel about what Butch's mother just said,? Obviously she is upset. How do you feel about this mother's pain?" Geraldo queried Miss Browning. Don't y'all kno' that brazen wench sat there with a straight face and said, "I'm in love!" Geraldo, who has had the dysfunctional, dispossessed, despised, disenfranchised, disadvantaged, the dissed 'n' the disobedient on his show, has heard and seen it all. But this took the cake. Geraldo's shoulders slumped, when Butch piped up, and lookin' in his teacher's eyes, said, "I love this woman. I want to marry her. I will finish school. I will get a job and take care of her. We will raise a family. No other woman can satisfy me like Belinda." Geraldo was speechless, which is unusual for him, and the audience groaned.

Butch's mother, in a state of absolute exasperation, looked at her skinny, puny, little offspring and asked, "Son, what do you mean Belinda is the only woman who can satisfy you? How long have you been having sex, since you were ten?" Butch looked at his mother like she was crazy and said, "Ma, you know that ten years old is too young for a child to have sex!" SILENCE!!!

Geraldo's face dropped, his shoulders slumped even further, said, "TEACHERS WHO SAY THEY ARE IN LOVE WITH THEIR STUDENTS is the focus of this edition of 'Geraldo'. Stay tuned, we will be right back."

After the show, Butch, Belinda and Butch's momma Barbara were beseiged by book publishers, movie and t v. producers, tabloids and magazine news shows, all salivating with fists full of money, vying for the rights to this sad, sorry saga. Belinda the teacher and Butch's momma Barbara busied themselves signing contracts as Butch stood by sucking his thumb 'n' lookin' confused. Dirt sells these days faster than Fanny Flanagan the French fan dancer fanned her naked fanny with a fan made of feathers in club flamingo. I can talk about ugly all night long.

Today, society is riddled with scandals, schemes, 'n' slime that slides beneath the scales of decency, and down the slimey, slippery slopes of shame, leavin' lives in shambles and shakin' the shingles of sanity as decent people watch stunned, as those in high places engage shamelessly in shady deals, sex, slander, shilly-shally, and other salacious shenanigans.

Today, anything may come outta people's mouth. Take, for instance, the case of New York's junior GOP Senator (pot hole) Al D'Amato, who is always up the river fishin' in Whitewater. It will be interesting to see what he catches. Back to my point: Senator Al's lips flew open on a N.Y. radio show where he attempted to lampoon Judge Ito's Japanese accent, which the judge doesn't have. All of a sudden, the Senator came to his senses, at least he appeared to have. He grabbed a full plate of crow, shagged ass back to Capitol Hill, stood on the senate floor, and commenced to gorge himself on his own asininity, apologizin' for his addledpated outburst, which took the cake and a few other pastries. "I am sorry, blah, blah, blah."

These kind of scatter-brained outbursts constantly issue from the lips of those in positions of supposed dignity, which in my unlettered view should reflect decorum, class and statesmanship. Instead, some public officials comport themselves on the level of shock jock Howard Stern. What kind of example is this for our youth? Ugly, that's what it is, ugly: Don't people know that loose lips sink ships?

Speakin' of loose lips, the king of loose lips himself, whom I have raked across the coals on several occasions is none other than (How am I doing?) Ed Koch, who has rubbed more people the wrong way than a Brillo pad. When Ed was New York City's Mayor, his lips ran amuck like wild horses. When the voters could no longer relish Ed's crazy talk, they told him to take a walk; a long walk, we had hoped, off of a short pier, into the deep waters of silence. But alas! Our hopes were short lived. Ed continues to pop up everywhere, on t.v., selling insurance, books, in commercials, editorials, radio, spokesperson for whatever, and the New York Post. We are constantly bombarded by his shrill opinionated utterances.

When this amateur actor was playin' New York City's Mayor, he dressed himself in a chicken suit, donned an afro wig and engaged in other wild antics. It's impossible to get rid of Ed Koch. He is like Fu Manchu: he keeps on comin' back. In my unlettered opinion, Koch is conceited and belligerent. His cantankerous, analyzing balderdash constantly stirs the ill winds of controversy, as the mainstream news organs, both print and electronic, feed like ferocious birds upon every devisive word that drops from Ed's lips. Koch's lips should be given a speedin' ticket. His bellicosity causes Mayor Giuliani to have nightmares 'n' daymares too!

The bottom line is if you want to be rich and famous these days, show your ass or say crazy shit out of your mouth. Of course, it pays to be of the right 'persuasion', if you know what I mean.

The crowd once again came to their feet, and woof-woofed and high fived each other. "Kick ass Sweetman," someone yelled out. Sweetman motioned to the crowd to sit down. I'll talk 'bout ugly all night, Sweetman continued.

The judge said to me, "Are you finished?" No! I said, I got a whole lot mo' ugly shit to talk 'bout. Naw take politicians and bureaucrats. Trying to git a straight answer from them is like tryin' to find teeth in Mother Carye's chicken's mouth. The minute that you think they are being straight with you—bang! They scaterlate the aberlum and humpharble the hockermettus, and tell you it is cloudy on a clear day. At election time we vote them in office. No sooner than they are in, they tell us to kiss their fanny, as they steal, live high on the hog, mismanage, embezzle, 'n' what not.

Then comes time for re-election. We the voters sleepwalk to the polls and vote them back in office, so they can rob us again and tell us we must bear the pain, as the hounds of budgetary gloom howl like hellish demons from hell; and the President, governors and mayors around the country, wear the dreaded cloak of recession, and watch like Dracula as the vampire bats of depression sink their fangs into the taxpayer's wallets, causin' us to howl in financial pain.

Looking grim at press conferences, politicians wax verbose and double speak in grave tones as they explain how we must, "bear the pain." Upon hearin' this criddley-crap, taxpayers groan, like a hound without a bone, and howl and bay at the unbalanced budgetary moon, which is obscured by the dark clouds of fiscal restraint.

The politicians tell us we must tighten our belts. How are we the taxpayers goin' to tighten our belts, when we don't have enough money to buy one. Our trousers are fallin' down around our ankles, exposing our bare ass(ets), such as we may have left after taxes.

My fellow Americans, wake up! The days of wine 'n' roses are over. The good ol' days are gone and the days of bread and water are upon us! This country has gone from sugar to—shucks. Oh I tell you it is ugly.

Banks and financial institutions are foldin' faster than the accordion played by Steve Urkell. Taxes and the cost of living are escalating higher than the miniskirt of a low priced hooker. The economy is sinkin' lower than alligator infested swamp land in Orlando, as politicians' lips continue to move faster than the wings of a fruit fly in a orange grove in Florida.

Ugly, the mess that's happening today is so ugly. People are confused as a purple pole cat dancing the polka in Poland, eatin' a hot pickled Polish pickle in the pourin' purple rain. If this don't leav' yo' hobblestruck. I don't kno' what will.

Mull this: Not long ago, I witnessed a multiloquacious scappernacious scuttlescrap that came from the mouth of a prominent Republican, Congressman Richard Dogooder (known on Capitol Hill as Slick Rick, friend of former President Tricky Dicky), who was being interviewed on the Sunday morning t.v. program, FACE THE PEOPLE, with anchor Gabe Perlmutter, who interviewed the Congressman on the state of the economy and the fact that he was under investigation for numerous improprieties. This is what came from betwixt his glib lips.

"Gabe", the Congressman said, "in my opinion government must first cap spending and index capital gains and on the tail of that of course we must increase exports and decrease imports which may rub the Japs the wrong way, causing them to squawk, of course this is to be expected from those people. Nonetheless, in my estimation this move would stimulate our sagging economy, which is basically healthy in spite of the economic slump, but which is suffering from a severe case of fiscal flu, which could be cured with a hot cup of stringent budgetary tea and monetary rest.

"Our next move, Gabe, and this is a crucial one: give a 'goose' to the gross national product, of course first taking into account the current fiscal mood of the international monetary market, which would rally our slumping stock market, lower prices in the supermarket, and allow more Oriental fish markets in the colored neighborhoods, thus giving the slumping economy a much need shot in the arm, causing the down side to swing upward, heading off a recession or depression, whichever may be visited upon the American taxpayer first.

"Of course, the American people must (here we go again) bear the pain, which will disappear with a sound fiscal rub down, which will cause an upswing in interest rates on CDs, T-notes, personal savings, money market accounts, and other investment products.

"In spite of the doom and gloom of nay sayers in the Democratic Party, our economy is not chronically ill and a secondary diagnostic operation is unnecessary. However, I'm calling upon Democratics and Republicans in the House to put aside partisan politics and let's put our collective noses to the fiscal grindingstone, which will be painful. I cannot stress this salient point too strongly—it's imperative that we, as God-fearing Americans, grasp the fiscal bull by the horns, which could be dangerous, and take without fear the budgetary cow by the tail, which could be messy. Nonetheless, we must or we could find ourselves on the horns of a fiscal dilemma, if a damper is not put on the deficit."

Gabe...by this time was in a state of great annoyance, having not been able to get a word in edge wise on his own show, took umbrage at the Congressman's ramblin' loquacious middlequiddle that was in a word incongruous, to say the least. "Congressman please!" Gabe said, "We are about out of time. I have a couple of quick questions I would like for you to address. First, you have received a great deal of criticism from various quarters, including you colleagues, regarding your stringent views on such issues as abortion, infidelity, family values and, especially, gangsta rap. And second, rumors are afoot that you are being investigated for sexual misconduct and misappropriation of Congressional funds, by The House Ethics Committee. Would you please comment?"

"I would be delighted to Gabe," the Congressman said. "As a righteous man I take strong demurral to these scurrilous politically movitated allegations. As to your first inquiry, yes, I am a staunch believer in marital fidelity, honesty, and a deep abiding love for God, the sanctity of life, family values, and this great country of ours, which is built upon the bedrock of Christian principles (what a crock), which I am proud to champion.

"God Bless America!" The Congressman got besides himself and broke into song, *Oh beautiful for spacious skies and amber wa....* "Congressman Dogooder, we don't have time for this sh..., I mean we only have a few moments for you to answer my last questions," Gabe, the show's host, snapped.

"I'm sorry Gabe, but this great country of ours means so much to me. I have been blessed and I'm sure you have too, Gabe. I have two wonderful children, who have never given me a moment's problem. A wife, who knows her place is at home, and a constituency that has kept me in office for twenty years, and I expect to be re-elected come election time. Let me say this Gabe," Congressman Dogooder threw up both hands preventing Gabe from cutting in. "Gangsta rap is an eroding cancer that is eating away at the very moral fabric of our youth's minds, causing a demoralizing decline in our society.

"I'm introducing a bill in Congress, that will make this kind of music—if you can call it that—this debasing type of tripe illegal to be performed, sold, or even recorded. Gabe, we need more culturally uplifting groups like Guns 'n' Roses, The Grateful Dead, The Sex Pistols or The Buzzcocks, not this depraved gangsta rap, that those people do. What's gotten into them Gabe?"

"There was a time when the nig—I mean coloreds—were happy. Naw days, they've gotten uppity and no longer know their place. That's why they're singing those crazy violent rap songs. After all we have done for those people they are turning on us. What we must do Gabe, is go back to the good old days, when we would whip their a—" The Congressman caught himself. Gabe was sweating bullets. Oh Shit, if this fool keeps running his mouth, Al Sharpton will be all over my ass, Gabe thought to himself. Gabe cut in before the Congressman could continue and said, "Congressman Dogooder, we are out of time. It has been good having you on the show this morning. I hope you can come back soon." (Gabe lied.) The Congressman departed the studio, skirting the questions of stealing and sexual impropriety.

Well wouldn't you know the very next day the lead story on the six-o'clock news and emblazoned across the front page of every newspaper across America was "WELL KNOWN CONGRESSMAN BUSTED!" CONGRESSMAN DOOGOODER CAUGHT IN TRYST! etc...The stories went on to say that Congressman Doogooder was caught with his drawers down engaging in carnal relations with a girl younger than his daughter (who is sixteen) in a Washington, D.C. 'ho' house, oops, I mean Hotel. The same Hotel where Dick (toe suckin') Morris (President Clinton's former political stragietist) was caught. That's a busy hotel. With the hair from the girls lower quarters wedged between his teeth, the Congressman pulled up his drawers 'n' waxed lugubrious and commenced to explain his unvirtuous actions. He muttered some ludicrous nonsense: "She tricked me. I'm overworked! (I would say so) I didn't know what I was doing! She set me up! The devil made me do it! Blah, blah, blah..." the Congressman mumbled. Ugly!!! I could talk 'bout it all night long.

Congressman Dogooder summoned his high-priced lawyer and gathered his dysfunctional family, who rallied to his side, projecting a picture of solidarity and went before a press conference of muckmongers 'n' news persons to explain the circumstances under which he was caught with his drawers down and his tongue out.

The Congressman's expensive mouthpiece spoke: "My client is innocent of these scurrilous allegations, which are nothing more than a politically motivated attempt to smear the Congressman," intoned the lawyer with the air of a holy man. He added, "As a result of these false charges, the Congressman has been under tremendous strain and is *non compis mentis*. Therefore, ladies and gentlemen, my client will make a brief statement and will take no questions. Congressman." The lawyer stepped back from the bank of microphones.

The Congressman stepped forward, enrobed in the garment of contrition. That sophistical jack ass, that…that…sorry rakehell wept.—This is ugly!—He wept as he read from a prepared statement. "I'm sorry." (I'm sure we have heard that one before.) "Forgive me. I apologize to my family (looking at his wacked out wife, son and daughter) and my constituency for my lapse in judgement. I pray that you will find it in your hearts to forgive me. God has. The Bible tells us to forgive one another. I'm sorry. Thank you." Ain't this a fiddlersbitch.

Clutchin' the Bible, the Congressman stepped back. His wife Dorothy Dixon-Dogooder, a long sufferin' woman, heavily under the influence of Prozac, Valium, and alcohol, stepped up to the bank of microphones and television cameras in a crapulous state, looked into the cameras, then up at her whoremonger of a husband, who has screwed man, woman, and child. Wearin' dark glassed to hide her shame, pain, 'n' bloodshot eyes, with slurred speech, said, "I love my husband. He is a good man. I will stand by him like Mary Jo Buttafuoco stands by her Joey," she mumbled, as her lust ridden, lyin', double speakin', sticky fingered, hypocrite of a husband stood there lookin' as sincere as a church deacon—oops! This may not be a good example.—Well, anyway.

Mrs. Dorothy Dixon-Dogooder havin' finished her ramblin' prattle, stepped back from the cameras and gave her husband a feeble smile. The Congressman's lawyer stepped forward. "That's all folks! No questions," he said. After the press conference was concluded, the Congressman and his wacko family were surrounded by heavy security, who hustled them into their sleek, black, chrome-trimmed stretch limo, with tinted windows. As the limo pulled away, hoards of crazed paparazzi and muckmongers 'n' mongeresses chased it like a hoard of wild dogs chasin' a fat wart hog through the wilderness, tryin' to be the first to get the dirt to dish.

Lady Flo (Going With The Flow) Anthony, the gossipmongeress and the queen of muck 'n' mire, Cindy Adams (New York Post) locked horns. Flo, being that she was a friend of the Dogooders, was invited to ride in the limo with the assurance that she would be given the real scoop. Not to be outdone, Cindy bogarded her way into the limo. Well, just let me tell you, both Flo and Cindy got more than they were expecting. All hell broke loose!

Long sufferin' Dorothy Dixon-Dogooder, who was in the grip of Toxic Psychosis, brought on by Prozac 'n' Valium, washed down with alcohol—a concoction that would cause King Kong to go wack 'n' bug out—screamed, "YOU BASTARD! You loose dick son-of-a-bitch! I hate you! You, you, yo—, piece of shit from hell," shrieked the Congressman's wife, causin' Flo 'n' Cindy to almost jump out of the limo. However, they composed themselves, quickly. With pens poised over pads and tape recorders runnin', they were ready to catch every bit of dirt 'n' lint that was about to drip, drop, 'n' transpire in the limo on that fateful day. Dorothy Dixon-Dogooder did not disappoint. The two premier Queens of gossip got an ear 'n' eye full.

"You loose dick son-of-a-bitch," blurted Dorothy, lookin' at her husband the Congressman as though she wanted to kill him. She sputtered, "I have, you, you…ha…ha…blitch, blask, bastard! You...hoove, have messed up all of our lives in this flamby...fam...family. I have stood by your side, a…a    faithful    wife    and    watched    you,    let    you, you…you…you…abuss…abuse me and the children. Look at them, you piece of filth! They aren't fit for shit, because of your abusive, skirt chasing, power crazed ass. Our lives are ruined!" Dorothy was on a roll—"All these years, long painful years, I have put up with your bull shit. If it weren't for me, you wouldn't amount to shit!" Dorothy Dixon-Dogooder shouted at her husband.

"SHUT UP!" The Congressman shouted at his wife, as he raised his hand to strike her.

"You bastard, you foul son-of-a-bitch. If you ever raise your hand or voice to me again. If you do, I will do something to you that the Almighty or the devil, has never heard of, or have a name for," shouted Dorothy, lookin' at her husband as though she was about to kill 'em. The Congressman not knowin' what had come over his wife lowered his hand and slid further away from her, fearin' she would do some ungodly thing to him.

The two children sat mute, looking like creatures from space. "Look at your children," shrieked Mrs. Dogooder. "They aren't fit for nothing, thanks to you." She continued her tirade as she stared at her husband. "Our son is a drugged up jellyfish. Our daughter is shacking up with a Black gangsta rapper. While you with your hypocritical ass yak about rap music and gangsta rappers, our lilly white daughter is bedded down with one. Oh! What's a white woman to do? I wish someone would run off with me. At least I would be rid of your low-lifed ass!" The Congressman sat silent. "Give me another drink," Mrs. Dogooder demanded. "You don't need another drink my darling," the Congressman said, meekly. "Don't darling me, you...you," stuttered Mrs. Dogooder, searching for another dirty word to call the Congressman but one wouldn't come to mind. She continued, "What in hell do you know what I need? You haven't taken care of my needs in years. If it weren't for the milkman, t.v. repairman, delivery man, and any other man, my needs would have been neglected."

Mrs. Dorothy Dixon-Dogooder downed her drink, poured herself another, and popped a Prozac 'n' several more Valiums. Flo and Cindy watched aghast as Dorothy washed the pills down with a glass of scotch. These two ladies of the mess—oops, I mean press—who have seen 'n' heard it all and can spot microscopic particles of dirt in the dark of night, wrote feverishly in order to capture the very essence of the *jimjams* that was emergin' before their eyes. The ladies were writin' at such a pace, they both developed cramps in their hands at the same time, causin' them to cry out in unison, "Hand don't you dare start no shit now." The cramps backed up and their hands continued to scribe feverishly, as the sleek black limo glided gracefully towards its destination, the outskirts of Washington, D.C., where the rich, powerful, the mighty and, in many cases, the libertine and morbiferous (lets go to the dictionary) live in splendor. The Dogooders resided in such deceptive surroundings, their wretched lives hidden from public scrutiny behind a facade of opulence and rectitude. Back in the limo, Dorothy Dixon-Dogooder poured herself yet another drink, much to the consternation of the others in the car. No one dared say a word. Silence...

The daughter stared out of the window as though what was going on in the limo was quite natural. The son, Slick Rick Jr., stared into the roof of the limo with a crazed look on his face as he conversed with aliens from far off. The Congressman sat speechless, which is quite unusual for a politician whose mouth is always runnin'. With baited breath, Flo 'n' Cindy, with pens poised over their note pads, waited. Silence...

Without warning: "Scumbag!" Screamed Dorothy. She flung her drink in her husband's face. He cringed, but remained silent. The only sounds to be heard were the purrin' of the limo's motor and Flo 'n' Cindy's pens as they moved across the pages of their notepads. They looked at each other, then at Dorothy, as she descended further into a state of *doloroum*.

Dorothy leaned forward, pressed a button—"Tom", she said with slurred speech, addressin' the chauffeur. "Yes'um Miss Daisy, I mean Miss Dorothy." She continued, "Tom I want you to know how much you have meant to me. What is it now Tom, twenty-five years?" "Yes'um" brother Tom answered. Dorothy continued, "Thomas dear, you have been my Tom cat and best friend. If it weren't for you, I would have forgotten what it feels like to be a woman." The Congressman, wiping the drink from his face that Dorothy threw on him, stared at her surprised, but dared not open his mouth. Dorothy ranted on, "Tom." "Yes'um," Tom responded, havin' turned a shade blacker, "Over the years, we became close, remember when we drove up the coast, just me and you and we..." "Go on naw, Miss Dorothy, don't fret yo'se'f non', Lordy, Lordy, Lord," blurted Tom, cuttin' Miss Dorothy off befo' she spilled the beans 'n' a few other vegetables—or let a wild cat out of the bag—but it was too late. "Oh shit!! This bitch is goin' crazy 'n' go' git me fucked up," thought Tom to himself, who by this time had turned completely white 'n' his lips were hangin' open like a wuff's pussy 'n' fo' pounds o' liver.

Upon hearing this juicy revelation, Cindy Adams bolted upright, surprised, and the hairs on her sable coat stood up, but the look on Flo's face said, "I knew it all along." Brother Thomas was stiff as a board 'n' looked like the first cousin of a ghost. Dorothy Dogooder started to shake as though she was operatin' a jack hammer, "Bastard," she screeched one last time at the Congressman. Her wig slid over to the left hand side, her make-up was in the process of dissipation. Mucilage rushed forth from her flared nostrils. She spoke in a' incoherent tongue as she descended into a plangorous (let's go to the dictionary) condition and dissolved into *foundre en larmes*. Dorothy Dogooder's wig fell off. Her eyes wide 'n' glazed, she slumped back into her seat in a complete state of hugger-mugger and waxed mad as a March Hare, her condition brought on by her husband's ingloriousness—com'on you kno' what to do!

The limo from hell pulled up to the Dogooder's estate. Brother Thomas jumped outta the car lookin' like he had had a glimpse of hell and ran off like a distracted man. He didn't even bother to open the limo door for his passengers. He left Miss Dorothy 'n' the others on their own.

Cindy 'n' Flo alighted from the limo with due haste, grabbed a cab, 'n' hopped a flight back to New York, to yak, yak on Geraldo Rivera's weekly celebrity yakfest. When the plane touched down at J.F.K. Airport, Geraldo Rivera and a gaggle of daytime talk show host were waitin', hopin' to book Cindy 'n' Flo on their shows (except Oprah, who was in Texas, settling a Mad-Cow beef). Geraldo almost knocked Sally down as he husseled Flo and Cindy into a waiting helecopter. Thinkin' quick on her feet, Sally cried out "Look! Geraldo, there goes O.J. Simpson." "Don't toy with me, Sally," said Geraldo. The mention of O.J. Simpson sends Geraldo into spasms of daytime hugger-mugger.

Dorothy Dixon-Dogooder was committed to a fruit factory—oops, I must be politically correct—what I mean is an institution for the emotionally frazzled. The Dogooder children continued their tumble-down way of life. The son continued to smoke crack 'n' talk to his friends from outerspace and sneak around with a married man. The daughter and the gangsta rapper broke up, and she married a politician, following in her mother's footsteps. The rapper continued composing gangsta rhymes. His latest CD, ZFUNKI-FUKINPOLITKZ, went platinum.

The young vulpine, with whom Congressman Doggoder was caught with his pants down, his teeth marks still fresh on her lower quarters, was besieged by talk shows and lucrative offers from book publishers and movie and television producers to tell of her lewd carryin' on's with her sugar daddy, Congressman Dogooder. That young voluptuous foxy-doxy gladly obliged 'n' became a' overnight media sensation 'n' rich to boot. The Congressman stood for re-election and won, as he predicted he would, because he knew that his sleep walkin', comatose constituents would march to the polls like sheep led to slaughter and vote him back into office, in spite of the fact that he had engaged in conduct unbecomin' for one in high office—or low, for that matter—and in spite of the fact that he was under investigation for other improprieties as well, which seem to make little difference in these days of instant redemption, apathy, and short memory.

What comes over some men, after they work hard to reach their lofty positions of respect and power? What is it that cause' them to stoop lower than alligator waste on the bottom of putrid swamp water in light of the fact that they are, in many cases, suave, have the looks of a movie star, sophisticated and are well educated? But once seduced by power, they wax egoric, become corrupt and arrogantly throw caution to the wind and thumb their noses at decency.

# Aubu

I recall a few years ago, a prominent Black Washington D.C. politician, who was not only well educated—the brother was smooth and street wise to boot—took leave of himself and ran headlong into the night like horny Harry hurryin' to the 'ho' house as he hurried to the hotel where his lady love awaited him.

Like a black widow spider, she invited him into her parlor "Come my love," she cooed. "Suck deep upon the pipe, the night is young." The door flew open, the trap was sprung—busted! "This can't be happening to me," he cried. "I'm the mayor of D.C. This is a set up! Racism, political harrassment, a vendetta against powerful Blackmen, blah, blah, blah."

This song is sung by every crook, thief, embezzler, drug seller, user, and power abuser, be they Black or White. White crooks when caught usually cry and com' down with amnesia. Black ones, when busted, wrap themselves in the tattered cloak of slavery and oppression and wear it like a burial shroud wrapped aroun' a corpse. True to form, the mayor was busted, jailed, released, and asked for and received instant redemption from his constituency, who voted him back into his former position. These sick, sorry sagas are played out on the political stage on a regular basis. UGLY!

When these men fall from power, pain and disgrace is visited upon their families, especially their long suffering wives, who have stood by their side, smilin' and endurin' their pain with regal fortitude, who are left to suffer alone as these roués in some cases continue their lecherous ways. However, men can and do change. Yesterday, I saw a leopard change its spots. Ha ha ha...oops! This is fodder for the comedians 'n' rhyme for da rappers.

# WOMEN'S LIB

*W*omen's lib started way back yonder, in the garden (When Adam and Eve were naked). Eve didn't feel like cookin' so she snatched a' apple from the apple tree 'n' tol' Adam, "Here, eat this!" The snake was hidin' in the bushes like snakes will do and slid in on his belly laughin', 'cause he had made Eve tempt Adam (who didn't need much persuadin') and put erotic notions in his head.

You may not be percipient of this fact, but the snake was the first peepin' tom on earth (hence snake in the grass). The snake was peepin' through the bushes with glazed eyes, watchin' what he had caused Adam 'n' Miss Eve to do. Today, people who like to watch are called peepin' Toms or Thomasinas. Out of this historical event emerged the phrase: *git down*, which has become a permanent fixture in the English language. When Adam bit into the fruit from the tree of good 'n' evil, he was standin' up. The apple havin' 'roused in him desires of a goatish nature, the words flew from betwixt his lips: "Woman, let's *git down!*"

Leave it to man to mess up a good thing—Sweetman abruptly cut short what he was about to say, shook his head, dabbed his lips with the red handkerchief, then reached into his bag and came out with a hand full of magic dust and threw it into the audience and uttered: *Uggamugga.*

The theater darkened for a moment, then the room became bathed in an amber colored glow. It seemed as though the light was issuing forth from the walls, floor and ceiling of the theater. Then music...a familiar song, very faint at first—I had heard that song before...where? It began to get louder—Yes! Naw I recall Big Joe Turner's, Shake Rattle 'n' Roll...*Git out dat bed wash yo' face 'n' han's, woman git in the kitchen mak' noise wit' da pots 'n' pans. Shake, Rattle 'n' Roll...*

Sweetman waved his *juju* stick and the music lowered and became the backdrop for Sweetman's consuposition on women's liberation. He continued: Back in the good ol' days a woman's place was in the home, cookin', washin', scrubbin', ironin', sewin', shoppin', tendin' the hearth as it were, havin' 'n' raisin' chullin'—usually a lot of 'em. After she labored all day, doin' womans' work, she was called upon to satisfy her man's need, which called for satisfaction constantly. When the man was in the high throes of incontinence, he would walk 'round the house hummin' Otis Redding's, "I Can't Get No Satisfaction."

*71*

The minute he walked through the do', he would holler, "Where's my supper, woman?" The little woman, or big momma (as the case may have been) would be standin' over a hot stove, her bosoms quiverin' over a hot pan of fried chicken 'n' a pot of steamin' collard greens, would stop what she was doin' and trot out of the kitchen like Edith Bunker to meet her man, 'n' say, "Honey, how was your day?" "Git away from me!" He would bellow, like Archie.

He would then rush straight to the supper table—didn't wash his hands—pile his plate high with food, eat like a hog and wouldn't say, "Thank you Lord or thank you honey." Finished, the man would then get up from the table, barely able to walk, go into the livin' room, flop his ass into his easy chair, like Archie Bunker, belch, break wind and holler, "Woman, bring me a cup of dat corn liquor."

The poor long-sufferin' wife would still be in the kitchen for hours with her hair standin' every which away all over her head, or her wig layin' over to the side, as she washed the supper dishes, wishin' her husband, or man (as the case may have been) would buy her a new dress, as she hummed Otis Redding's "Try a Little Tenderness." *Oh she may be weary, young girls, they do get weary wearin' the same ol' shabby dress, but when she gets weary, try a little tenderness.* "Woman!" The husband bellows from the bedroom, shatterin' his wife's musin'. "What' takin' you so long. Don't mak' me com' up in ther' 'n' git' you. My love don' come down, 'n' my hammer is up, 'n' daddy is ready to *git it on.*"

The little woman or big momma (as the case may have been) hurries from the kitchen to the bedroom, where her man had slapped another Otis Redding hit on the Victrola, "Rock Me Baby." *Rock me all night long. Jus' keep rockin' me baby, 'til my back ain't got no bone. Roll me, roll me baby like a wagon wheel, 'cause when you throw the roll on me, you don't kno' how you mak me feel.* Then they would commence to *git down* .

After about a minute 'n' half, he would let out a howl like a wart hog bein' kilt. I can't even 'scribe the kind of noise he would make. The po' woman would lay there in the dark 'n' go, "umph, umph, umph." And to add insult to injury, he would turn to her and say, "I laid a whuppin' on you, didn't I baby?" Then he would turn over and fall asleep 'n' snore like a' elephant, as a new life took form in her womb.

Before daybreak the little woman (or whatever) would attempt to git up 'n' go fix her man's breakfast, but not before he took his mornin' pleasure. Then he would lie there in bed on his ass until breakfast was ready. Umph, umph, umph!

Back yonder in them days, the women bent over backwards (when she wasn't on her back) to please her husband or man, but many men did not appreciate the woman's efforts. Some men were so insensitive they would stay out all night long, foolin', frolickin', fornicatin' 'n' what not, and would come slidin' like a snake into the house somewhere in the wee hours of the mornin', or in some cases days later, broke 'n' funky as a goat. Bleatin' 'n' bellowin' all kinds of crazy shit. "Bitch, where is my dinner," he hollers. Naw keep in mind, he has been away from home for days. "You hear me talkin' to you," he bellows. "I'm sorry," says the little woman or big momma (as the case may have been).

The man would commence to talk all kinds of crazy shit that made no sense at all. In his insensitive drunkeness, he would lay upon his faithful wife what Ike Turner laid upon Tina, and to add insult to injury he would hum that part of Big Joe Turner's song "Shake, Rattle 'n' Roll" that went, *You're like a one eyed cat, peepin' in a seafood store. I can look at you woman 'n' tell you ain't no child no mo'*. Ugly, umph!

Well, women got tired of bein' beat, broke, battered, 'n' bearin' babies for the brute. She got tired of searchin' in the carpet, under the bed 'n' couch for her teeth 'n' wig 'cause her man had gone crazy 'n' knocked them out, or off. So the women rose up 'n' rebelled 'n' left their asses faster than Tina left Ike. The taste of freedom caused some women to pull off their drawers 'n' bras 'n' set them afire and wear their skirts six inches shorter than a micro mini—you could see Christmas.

Case in point: A White woman by the name of Stella Stevens, got steamed at her abusive mate, Steven, who came home 'n' Stella hadn't started his supper. Steven slapped Stella. Stella slapped Steven back. Steven was taken aback. Steven snapped, "Bitch! Have you lost your mind?" "Slap me again and find out," snapped Stella. Steven stood stunned as Stella stuck a Virginia Slim in her mouth, took a long drag 'n' said, "I've come a long way, baby. No more working my ass off, then putting on a fucking black evening gown and singing some silly ass song about bacon frying in a pan." Shocked! Steven watched Stella stroll out of the house, with bare hooters bouncin' in the breeze like Madonna's. Stella's husband Steven was so shocked he came out of the closet 'n' married his boyfriend, Congressman Doogooder's son Tricky Rick Jr.

# Aubu

Meanwhile in Harlem, Tyesha Thompson, the wife of Thomas Thompson, went to the African House O' Hair' to get a Sengalese twist. While she was waiting to have blonde horse hair weaved into her naps, she picked up a copy of Essence Magazine and came upon the story of how Stella Stevens had liberated herself, got the notion to do likewise. Thomas, who whipped Tyesha every other day, was waitin' at the crib with his head bad off of reefer 'n' "NightTrain" for Tyesha to git home 'n' fix his dinner.

When Tyesha strutted through the do', Thomas yelled, "Bitch! Whar' you be'n?" Tyesha didn't answer. Thomas stood up. "Woman you must be cruisin' for a bruisin', achin' for a breakin'. I goin' to whup yo' ass," Thomas said, lungin' at Tyesha. She sidestepped him 'n' went up side of his head. Tyesha's blonde Senegalese twist was flyin' all over her head, here 'n' yonder. "Don't you ever call me a bitch, or put your hands on me again," said Tyesha. "If you do, I will do som' unlawful shit to yo' ass." "I'm sorry," mumbled Thomas meekly, rubbin' his head. The following two cases illustrate what can happen when a person or race of people has been driven to distraction after bein' subjected to physical and psychological abuse over a period of time and may be driven to exact extreme retribution upon the abuser.

I'm reminded of a story my momma used to tell about her great, great, great uncle Hezekiah, who was a slave: Uncle Hezekiah's massuh would whup 'em ever' day, 'cause he 'fused to shuffle, bow, rake, 'n' scrape. One day Uncle Heze said to his massuh, "Massuh ple's don' whup me no mo'. I's ti'ed uh bein' beat." Ol' massuh said, "Nigga is you sassin' me boy," and commenced to beat Uncle Heze real bad. Well suh, sumpin' came over Uncle Hezekiah, he grabbed de whup from ol' massuh's han' 'n' whupped ol' massuh so bad, he set Uncle Heze free. Next day ol' massuh hobbled to de field 'n' tol' de other slaves de was free too. Not bein' ones to look a gif' ho'se in de mouf, de took off 'n' ol' massuh commence to pick 'is own cotton." He was heard mumblin', "I don't want to see another nigger as long as I live."

This case is a lulu: A white man by the name of John Wayne Bobbitt, the husband of Lorena, who had committed violence upon her person on a regular basis, got out of bed one night and went into the bathroom to pee. Somethin' was missin', but he couldn't put his hand on it. He went back to bed. Finally it dawned on him what it was that was missin'. "Oh Shit!" he screamed, "it's gone—my thing (such as it was) is gone. Lorena don' cut it off!"

Meanwhile, drivin' wildly through the night, Lorena clutched somethin' in her hand. She knew that it felt familiar, but for the life of her, she couldn't put her finger on it. It dawned on her after a while, what it was. She screamed—and threw it out of the car window and it landed in the bushes.

Meanwhile, back at the Bobbitt house, John called 911 to report his missin' part. A search team of gay police persons were called in to hunt for "it". They frantically beat the bushes in search of "it". After a short while one of the officers yelled, "I got it." (Com' on people git your mind out of the gutter.) They rushed it to the hospital where a team of surgeons reunited John Bobbitt with his pecker.

The news of this sorry event spread 'roun' the world like wildfire. Dirtmeisters, gossipmongeress, tabloids, and talk shows ran over each other like crazed cats in a patch of catnip, as men who had been less than prudent began sleepin' on their stomachs with their legs tightly closed. Oh my goodness! Before the stitches were removed from John's reattached pecker, the talk shows received him with open arms. Crazed women in the studio audience volunteered to help John test his reattached ding-a-ling to see if it still worked. This scoundrel made enough money to buy himself a state-of-the-art pecker. The last I hear tell he had stopped slinging his pecker and gone to preachin'. Lorena Bobbitt established a 900 psychic hotline, where scores of women call her for advice. I wonder what kind.

Now I am going to *tongue lash* (Sweetman dabs his lips) you women. Umph! 'Cause som' of you have had good men, who loved 'n' cherished you, put you up on a pedestrian or whatever—but you were less than chaste and did not appreciate it 'n' carried on like a wild wench 'n' a loose hussy, throwin' your drawers hear 'n' yonder and flingin' yo' limbs asunder, allowin' another, other than your main man or husband, to slide betwixt your quarters 'n' ride you like a cowboy rides a wild mare at the County Fair. Umph, umph, umph!!

Case in point: I kno' of a woman who lived down yonder in Everywhichaway. She had a good husband 'n' she had three boyfriends. One boyfriend was named Fuzzy. One was named Such-As-That. The third one was called Some-Of-Them. One mornin' her husband left for work. He kissed her 'n' said: "I'll see you this evenin', honey. Have a good day. I love you." "You have a good day too 'n' I love you," she lied. The husband wasn't out of the house more than half 'n' hour when the door bell rang—ding-a-ling. The lady answered the do'. It was Fuzzy, comin' to call. "Baby, I saw yo' husband leave so I came right over. We got all day. I'm goin' to rock yo' world," bragged Fuzzy. "Com' on rock it," she said. They went into the bedroom 'n' was 'gittin' down', when the door bell rang—ding-a-ling. "Damn," she said, "Fuzzy quick! Hide under the bed." Fuzzy got up under the bed. The lady answered the do'. It was Such-As-That. "Baby, I kno' yo' husband is at work, so I came by to git me a piece," said Such-As-That. "You kno' you can git it, com' on in the bedroom," she said. They commenced to git down—way down. The do' bell rang—ding-a-ling. "Such-As-That! Hurry! Hide in the closet," the lady said.

She went 'n' answered the do'. It was Some-Of-Them. "Oooh wee, momma, you sho-nuff is lookin' good, umph, umph, umph," said Some-Of-Them. "I kno' yo' ol' man is at work 'n' I'm off today, so I came by to lay a whuppin' on you," he added. "Well, don' stan' there in the do', com' in 'n' git busy'," she said. They went into the bedroom 'n' commenced to moan, groan, 'n' grind, causin' Fuzzy under the bed 'n' Such-As-That in the closet to engage in edeogargalismus, self-pleasuring—if you will.

Click, click—the sound of a key turnin' in the tumbler. "Oh Shit!" The lady let out a muffled cry. "My husband is home. Hurry, Some-Of-Them, run up stairs 'n' hide." Some-Of-Them grabbed his pants 'n' drawers 'n' ran upstairs. The lady hurried 'n' sprayed the room with "Mist of Lust" air freshener 'n' laid back on the bed with her legs agape, lookin' all sexy. Her husband came into the bedroom. "Honey I got off early today, I' goin' to lay a hurtin' on you," he said, not yet realizin' that she had already had three hurtin's laid upon her. He looked up betwixt her agape quarters 'n' said: "Oooh wee, I see fuzzy." Fuzzy jumped up from under the bed 'n' ran out of the house. Surprised, the husband said, "Honey, you allow such as that in here." Such-As-That, broke out of the closet 'n' ran pass the husband. He grabbed his shotgun 'n' said, "Dammit! I'll git some of them," Some-Of-Them jumped out of the upstairs window 'n' broke his neck.

I got to tell on myself. Let me share with you my experience 'n' amorous episodes. Durin' my time, I've thrown my trousers over many a bed post from Frisco to Philly. Therefore, I can identify with what it's like for the lady's husband to come home early 'n' I had to depart in a hurry, leavin' my trousers behind. I have gunshot wounds to prove it. I supposed it could have been worse. One day a lady's husband came home 'n' there was a pair of pants on the floor at the foot of the bed. The husband knew that they didn't belong to him. He looked in the closet, and there stood a naked man. So the husband shot the naked man. It could have been worse! Then the husband went over to the bed 'n' shot his wife. It could have been worst! Then the husband put the pistol to his head 'n' shot himself. It could have been worse! If he had looked under the bed, he would have seen me. An oldie but a goodie!

# HAIR MANIA

*E*verybody don' gon' hair crazy naw days. It's a' ugly sight to see White children, runnin' 'roun' tryin' to look hip-hop, hoppin' up 'n' down the street with their wrinkled no-name brand jeans hangin' off of their skinny asses. Dirty sneakers. Patches of hair stickin' up on their heads, that look as though a wild bird had lit 'n' went wack.—The mostly Black audience leaped to their feet. Some rolled in the aisles. Their laughter shook the rafters. They woof-woofed and high fived each other.

"Shut up 'n' sit still, no need for y'all to laugh at nobody. I'm comin' to you next," said Sweetman. "Oh Shit," said a young man who sported a hairdo from hell, that would make Coolio's look tame. Sweetman pointed to the young man and said, "Lord have mercy! Boy, look at yo' head. I never thought I would live to see naps waxed 'n' stickin' up in the air. Damn, man, your head looks like a pin cushion. Some of you out there got so many parts in your heads, it looks as though trains ran across them in different directions. Some look like patches of grass growin' on a bowlin' ball."

Moving with the grace of a ballet dancer, Sweetman moves to the edge of the stage and points his finger at the young man with the hellish hair-do and said, "Stop all this hair foolishness 'n' git yo' se'f a sensible hair cut." With that he reaches up and snatches off his wig, exposing his bald head, with two moussed patches of hair on each side that stood up like the devil's horns. Standing with his right hand on his hip and the wig dangling in the other, he raises it and waves it across the cheering crowd like a wand, or like the Pope bestowing a blessing.

Sweetman drops the wig into his bag and comes out with a can of hair spray, sprays his horns, drops the can back into the bag, then stands with his face expressionless, giving the crowd a few moments to compose themselves. He continues—Mess, mess all over the world. All this hair mess. Everybody is runnin' 'roun' trying to git some hair. Some people are not satisfied with the hair the Lord gave 'em. As I look out over this assemblage this evening I see only two women with their own hair. All the rest is store bought. Hair mania has swept America. Hair is in such demand, the N.Y. Amsterdam News has run out of advertising space in the classified section of the paper.

Sisters in Africa got wind of the money that could be made in Harlem braidin' hair. They got on the first boat smokin out of Africa. It seems that we Black people will never learn our lesson about gettin' on boats. Brothers 'n' sisters will flock to the waterfront 'n' pay to go on a boat 'n' ride 'roun' Manhattan. There ain't no tellin' where you could wind up. Ha ha ha, umph! Oh well, anyway, no sooner than the boat from Africa docked in the U.S.A., the African sisters ran to 125th Street 'n' set up hair parlors, causin' som' domestic sisters to git hot under the curlin' iron and their sto' bought braids. Before sun up, from St. Nicholas Avenue to Adam Clayton Powell Jr. Boulevard in Harlem the hair braidin' sisters line 125th Street, with their portfolios open displayin' the different ways they can style 'n' braid hair.

They can also be an aggressive lot. I saw a lady com' up out of the subway, turn the corner on 125th Street with her hair undone. A group of African hair braidin' sisters spotted her. They descended upon the poor woman and braided her hair while she loudly protested. These hair braidin' sisters mean business. They will braid *anything* that has hair on it.

You may not believe this, but it is true. I saw them chase a pit bull, catch it, and braid its hair, as the poor animal lay there afraid to move—it stood in the middle of the street 'n' let itself be braided. Umph, umph, umph, ain't this a mess? From sun up 'til sun down, these hair braidin' joints are packed with women tryin' to git som' hair for their heads 'n' rats some for their nests.

Hair, hair, hair everywhere, Oh I do declare, what is this world comin' to? Whatever it is, I don't want to see it. Some of that store bought hair you women wear looks like braided rope, string, 'n'twine, sprayed different colors. I saw a woman in pursuit of hair go into Woolworth's department store to purchase som' hair, 'n' much to her displeasure she was informed by the sales clerk that Woolworth's was going out of business and their stock of hair was sold out. Well sir, that woman pitched a fiddler's bitch. "Goin' out of business, oh no you didn't, blah, blah, blah..." Not to be outdone, she purchased som' knittin' thread, cut it up 'n' glued it to her head. I kno' of another lady who was not satisfied with her natural hair, went into a Korean hair store, ordered ten pounds of blonde nappy hair and got mad as hell 'cause she couldn't pay for it with food stamps.

There was a time when you could buy a wig made of horse's hair. No more, Diana Ross took care of that. These days if a horse, mule, donkey, or any other animal with a mane sees her comin' they haul ass. Even lions don't take chances. They sleep with one eye open, just in case she shows up in the jungle singin' "Ain't No Mountain High Enough!"

A young girl came home from school and her mother was in the kitchen cookin' with her wig off, because of the heat. The child looked around bewildered, and said, "Excuse me, Miss, where is my mommy?"

I was watchin' t.v. in a store window 'n' saw a hip-hop commercial that went like this: "Yo, my name is hip Skip, President of the Hip-Hop Hair Club, for bald headed hip-hoppin' home boys. Is yo' hommies grinnin' 'cause yo' fade is thinnin'? Is yo' 'cess a mess? Is yo' do through? Is yo' 'fro 'bout to go? Don't sweat it, you ain't gots to be bald. Give us a call at 1-800-555-HAIR. We'll do, or re-do yo' do 'n' tighten yo' wig if it's too big. Dig it? Word. Don't delay, call today 'n' check out our complete line of home boy braids, fades, hair pieces, wigs 'n' toupees. We be havin' stupid hair for here (indicates heads), there (indicates chest) 'n' everywhere (indicates groin). Understand what I'm sayin?

"Our hip-hop transplants 'n' weaves are designed to withstand fire, floods, windstorms, and muggin's. With our secret (picks up a bottle of glue) scientific formula (puts glue on Styrofoam head) we can grow hair where hair (puts hair on Styrofoam head) has never grown befo'. Com' on money, pick up the phone 'n' call 1-800-555-HAIR. A trained staff of hip-hop homeboy hair care specialists are available to assist you and explain the misconception of muscatel (holds up wine bottle). Check us out G—we accept cash, checks, credit cards and food stamps. I'm not only the President of the Hip-Hop Hair Club, I'm also a hip-hop homeboy who usta be bald, Word up!"

Umph! Since the beginnin' of time there has always been this thing about good 'n' bad hair, continues Sweetman. Let me tell you how it all started: Everything was peaceful on earth, when there was just animals 'n' such. Animals weren't runnin' 'roun' talkin' that crazy hair jive. Dogs didn't go barkin', "bow wow wow", to the gorilla, "I got good hair, you got bad hair." Birds of the air didn't chirp 'bout good 'n' bad feathers, or straight 'n' nappy feathers.

This crazy hair foolishness started when the Creator decided to make man. To this day, he reponders that decision. Anyway, somewhere aroun' the sixth day, the Lord havin' made everything decided at the last minute to make the Blackman in his image. So he mixed up a batch of white clay, fashioned it into mankind and womankind too (you got to be careful in these days of political correctness).

Well anyway, the Lord placed the clay in the big oven to blacken, after which He would say, "Go forth 'n' multiply, be fruitful 'n' replenish the earth." The Black folk hurried forth to do just that. The Lord called out to the Black folk as they were hurryin' off to be fruitful. "Come back here", he said to the Black folk, "I forgot to put hair on your heads." Being that He was the shepherd, He called the black sheep unto himself and clipped their wool and put it on top of the Black folk heads.

When the Lord was finished, He said to them, "Go forth and don't forget to multiply." The Lord didn't have to tell them that twice. As a matter of fact, they were 'at it' befo' they came out of the oven. That's one commandment they haven't broken to this day. By now the Lord was weary, He had one more batch of clay to bake, and he slapped it into the oven and fell asleep and the fire went out.

When he awakened the next day and opened the oven, there was all those unbaked White people, so to expedite matters the Lord breathed the breath of life into them. Since the sheep had run off durin' the night and there were no lambs wool for their heads, the Lord looked down on the amber waves of grain, and from the corn fields he grabbed a hand full of corn silk and slapped it upon the White people's heads. "Naw git thee hence and multiply after your own kind." They went forth from the Lord with their hair blowin' in the wind and began to multiply after their kind and everybody else's. To this day some people don't know what color they are.

One day the White people were rummaging all over the land. They came upon a pastoral scene, where peace prevailed and Black people resided in idyllic splendor. A European brother by the name of Christopher said to another named Zeke, "Would you look yonder at that passle of pickaninnies with that nappy hair. Let's go 'n' say hello to them." The Black brothers 'n' sisters ran forth to greet their White brotherin'. "Come," they said. "Welcome to our homes. What's ours is yours, so please don't hesitate to help yourself to what you see." Well, the White people did jus' that. They commenced to help themselves and how.

Christopher said to Zeke, "Zeke, I got myself an idea. We need help on the plantation in America and those people, know how to cultivate the land. Jus' you look at those rice fields. Zeke, ol' buddy, if we took them to America, we would have amber waves of grain growin' in no time a'tall." "How is we go' git 'em to go wit' us?" asked Zeke. "I got a plan," said Chris. "If it don't work, we will beat their black asses 'n' make 'em go."

The European brothers were quick to perceive the value of workers already equipped with agrarian skills that would prove indispensable on the American plantation. So don't you never let no one tell you that the White man went to Africa and caught savages and brought them over here. Any fool will tell you that it would have reflected unfavorably on his bottom line. Another point of information before I go back to the main point of this story—hair.

Rice as well as other grains and crops were cultivated in Africa 'roun' the first millennium of the Christian Era. Wet rice (oryza glaberrima) was first domesticated on the middle Niger about 1500 B.C. with a secondary-*berceau*, or cradle between the Sine-Saloum and the Casamance Rivers. By A.D. 50, it was bein' cultivated at Jenn-Jeno, the oldest known Iron Age City in sub-Saharian Africa {See *Seeds of Change*, Smithsonian Institution Press}. So you can well see old Christopher knew what time it was.

Chris 'n' Zeke went to the head brother 'n' said, "You people got some funny hair, but that's not what we want to discuss with you at this time. To show our gratitude for your brotherly hospitality, we want to take you and your people on a boat ride. So go 'n' tell your people to pack rice, yams, goobers (peanuts), limes, peppers, okra, millet and sorghum." "If we are just goin' on a boat outin', why do we need to pack all of these provisions?" The head brother inquired. "Seems to me we're goin' on a permanent trip." "Oh no! Nig... no no! My brother, it's just a day trip, an outin' if you will, so that we may become better acquainted," said Christopher, winkin' at Zeke. Chris continued, "I thought we would take food and have a cookout and bar-be-cue. I know you people love ribs. "We don't eat ribs," said the head brother. "You will, as soon as we get you to Amer-Ah," said Chris, catchin' himself. "What I mean to say is we can eat, drink, and make merry, really get to know each other. We have a drink we want to share with you, it's called whiskey," said Chris.

The head brother reluctantly said, "OK, but we ain't down with all this mixin', minglin', eatin' pork, 'n' drinkin' whiskey jive, but I'll go along with the game." That was the damnest mistake he ever made.

Everybody piled on to the boat. The head brother thought to himself, "This is funny, why ain't the White woman gittin' up on da boat?" Before he could bring this to Christopher's attention, it was too late. Chains were being slapped on the Black folk. "Wut up wit' dis, Chris my man?" Said the head brother. "Jus' a game," said Chris. "We don't play this kinda shit," snapped the head brother. "You have never heard the Star Spangled Banner played either, but you will 'n' when you do yo' black ass will stand up," Chris snapped back. "N' another thing," said Chris. "From naw on, it's Master Chris! You got it boy?" The head brother started to protest, but thought better of it.

When the boat docked on these shores, children were gettin' off who weren't black 'n' they weren't exactlyy white. Their hair weren't straight 'n' it weren't nappy; in most cases it was somewhere in between and it would blow in the wind when the wind blew.

Since that day way back yonder, the good hair bad hair controversy has raged. Those brothers and sisters whose hair was not wind swept spent their every awaken moment, tryin' to make it do so. They're still at it to this day.

One day a sister by the name of Madam C.J. Walker, who possessed the gift of foresight, saw that there was a fortune to be made, upon observing the salient fact that a great number of her brethren 'n' sister girls wore rags on their head's, or in some form, fashion, or manner attempted to make their wooly locks curl or in som'wise become wind swept, because they experienced great mortification due to the texture of their natural endowment, which wouldn' blow in the wind when the wind blew.

Madam Walker smelt money in the wind 'n' made ready for the windfall. She got herself a large iron kettle 'n' mixed som' of this 'n' som' of that and concocted a concoction, a hair straightening process, which she called, Madam Walker's Hair Grower.

Those whose hair would not move even if a hurricane passed through flocked to Madam Walker in such numbers that she became the first Black female millionaire in America. {*Madam C.J. Walker*, by A'Lelia Perry Bundles, Chelsea House Publishers, New York, Phildelphia}

Madam Walker was a mover 'n' shaker durin' the Harlem Renaissance. This incongruous psychological hair disorder (skin color as well) is embedded in the deeper-most recesses of the subconscious mind of people of ebony 'n' alabaster lineage. Think 'bout this as I zig-zag 'n' segnuie to the followin.

# DON'T BUY THE HYPE

*I* will attempt to avoid waxing longwinded as I broach this next subject. You are intelligent people, umph! (Sweetman rolls his eyes. His expression says: Yeah, yeah right.) So you shouldn't have to eat a whole cow 'n' come down with mad cow (bovine spongiform encephalopathy) disease befo' you realize that you are eatin' beef—do you? Don't buy the hype, the melon may not be ripe. So be weary, what's goin' on naw days is scary. Be leery, my brother man and sister girl. You could get hurt, lose yo' shirt 'n' find yo' se'f walkin' naked in da hood.

Take it for what it's worth, it's not prudent to amble about through life in a somniferous state, but rather be punctilious at all times. Stop believin' everything you hear 'n' only half of what you see, it could lead to your undoin. Think for yo' se'f. If you don't there are those waitin' to do it for you, and you could wind up payin' 'em for their services. In these times, if you go through life with a walkman on yo' head 'n' yo' beeper 'n' your cel'phone ringing causin' your brain to take leave of its place of habitation you could find yo'se'f up the lazy river without a paddle.

Check out people, places 'n' things before you become involved with them—or go jumpin' in like a bull frog leapin' into a pond with no water—you could bus' yo' ass! Be careful of whom you invite into yo' house, they may trot off with yo' wife, husband, silverware, or plastic, depending upon your circumstances. In other words, look befo' you leap!

Only a fool will buy a pig in a poke. Open the bag 'n' check out what it is that you are payin' for. If you don't, you could be in for the shock of your life to discover that it's not a pig but a werewolf, that leaps up 'n' bites you in yo' ass, 'n' have you runnin' 'roun' talkin' shit 'bout, "I thought it was a pig." Pig my ass! It's too late then.

The Sweetman loves you, that's why I have come again to warn you of these negative goin's on's, in order that you may have the correct understandin', befo' you strapplelate the skittettus arrivin' at a' erroneous conclusion, then holler, "I assumed!" You would have the first three letters correct: ASS! So listen to me, so that you will not be a' ass—'Jack' or otherwise. In the words of James Brown (naw, that's a cautious man.) "Good gawd, git back, wait a minute. Looka here." Muse deep upon this.

I'm not a bibliomanian, (let's go to the dictionary) as many of you are. however, I'm blessed to be inspirited with mother wit coupled with street smarts, which gives me a particular instinct to decipher inborn patterns of activity and response commands to a given biological stock. What dafuk did I say? I've said a mouth full. By naw, however, you should have become cognizant of the fact that I'm given to loquacity and gibble-gabble and still be on the money, so, my beloved, roll what I jus' said 'roun' in yo' cranium, the instrument of your perspicacity and the meanin' of my scrapanacious scriddlescrapt will be visited upon your understandin.

Don't buy the hype, the melon may not be ripe. Have you heard the sayin', "Seein' is believin'"? Let me tell you it ain't necessarily so. For example, look aroun' you as you go about yo' daily activities. You will see people all dressed up, lookin' good and intelligent, but they are crazy as a bedbug! What I'm tryin' to say is, what you think you see may not be what you thought you saw.

Let me share with you a personal experience in this regard. Years ago, I was at a party—as a matter of fact, it was one of Madam Walker's chit'lin' 'n' champagne parties—where I met a fine, foxy lady. A vision of unearthly beauty. I asked her to dance, she obliged. We bumped, grinded, 'n' slow dragged. I was talkin' shit 'n' swappin' spit. I laid a yard of tongue upon her.

At evenings end, she invited me to her place for a nightcap, which weren't far from Madam Walker's. So I went, not one to turn down an offer from a young beautiful enchantress. As soon as we got inside of her apartment, she headed straight to the bedroom. I thought to myself: Damn, she's in a hurry. What about the nightcap? "Come" she cooed, beckonin' me to the bedroom. She kicked off her shoes, took off her hair, took off her bra, took off her breast, took off her drawers—and I took off!

Things are not always what they seem. So be wary, what's goin' these days, is scary. I recall some years back. Perhaps you do too. A deranged preacher, who had snakes in his boots 'n' bats in his belfry, and was twelve sermons short of the Holy Ghost, by the name of Jim Jones, persuaded thousands of lost, unthinkin' souls to follow him to their doom. He told them he had been "called" and if they would follow him into the jungle 'n' tabernacle with him he would serve them cold punch after the prayer meeting.

It's sad to say, but thousands of sleep-walkin' souls who would not, or could not, take responsibility to think their way out of a forest fire, and whose hearts thirsted for the soothin' waters of the Spirit, followed that crazy assed preacher into the bushes in South America and drank deeply of poisoned punch. I can assure you their thirst was quelled...permanently! For earthly water or otherwise.

Don't buy the hype, the melon may not be ripe. Don't take up 'n' follow everybody who says that they are"called"—"called" for what? It's sad and unfortunate naw days that so many people are blinded by their insatiable thirst for truth 'n' reason for being, they will follow anything or anyone who looks 'n' sounds Holy. You had better listen to The Sweetman.

In the words of the song sung by Sammy Davis Jr., "It Ain't Necessarily So." That's why I don't take as gospel everything that comes from the lips of man or woman, be they Black or White, light or bright, without sprinlklin' a box of salt 'n' a pound of pepper on it. You shouldn't either. My advice to you is this—take it or leave it—if someone is tryin' to sell you something and their lips are movin' faster than the hands of a dealer shufflin' cards in a three-card monte game, say "Slow down, Mr. Brown, hold up G., you are talkin' too fast for me—run it pass me again—slowly."

Don't be a sap 'n' buy the crap! Take for instance, you purchase a ticket to a concert with your hard-earned money. The singer's lips are movin', but they aren't singin', they're lip-synchin'. You gotta stand up 'n' say: "Yo, stop the show! Check this money, I ain't wack 'n' I ain't on crack, I want my money back."

Case in point: Remember a few years ago, those two long-haired Black lip-synchin', West Germans, Milli Vanilli, who lip-synched 'n' flim-flammed their way to fame 'n' fortune 'n' a Grammy award? I said it then, I'll say it again: *Ham hockin' der hagen dååzen snowlin es smitten globber burger, 'shin hike'n kliper un blazen huten glimmer'.* Simply put: *Auf Wiedersehem!*

What I say? Be alert. You could git hurt. If someone told you that they saw a clown, maybe they did, but it doesn't necessarily mean that the circus is in town.

Some people are so gullible that they are easily duped, cheated, taken to the cleaners even though their clothes aren't dirty. They allow themselves to be hoodwinked, fleeced, gulled, gyped, beguiled, deluded, tricked, bluffed, taken in, defrauded, victimized, bilked, diddled, flim-flammed, 'n' bamboozled. Naw ain't that a bummer, bitch, 'n' a few other things? There are those who are so mixed up they flip flop 'n' flock, grip 'n' grab on to anything 'n' anyone. As a consequence of this unthinkin' moonstruck behavior, hot house psychics have sprung up among us like fungus, and they are cleanin' up, as no-thinkin', sleepwalkin' people flock to them to be fleeced.

There are genuine psychics. President Franklin D. Roosevelt, consulted one, a Black woman; but you will not see psychics of that caliber on talk shows and in infomercials, prostitutin' their 'gifts' like a common concili-atrix, plyin' her (or his) wares on the 'ho' stroll. When you deal with TV psychics all you will get is a large phone bill from Ma Bell or somebody. Considerin' the complex issues facin' man 'n' womankind, it's no small wonder that so many people grab at any straw that floats on the waters of life, if they feel that it will bring them instant comfort and easement. Waitin' on the Lord is too slow for folks naw days.

Today's society, which is riddled with avarice 'n' greed, compels some people to take short cuts to fame 'n' fortune, and in some instances they will stoop lower than the tracks of a pit bull (that's low) in order to fulfill their inordinate ambitions and intemperate desires. These poor souls just want a' easier, softer way to solve complex issues such as love, marriage, family, and interpersonal relationships, which false prophets take advantage of and laugh all the way to the bank, leavin' them holdin' the bag—a' empty bag!

Listen to me people! In the early 1990's (or have you forgotten?), when Saddam Hussein, the so called Mad Man of Baghdad was causin' madness 'n' sayin' he was engaged in a Holy War. (If that was a holy war, I wonder what a' unholy one would be like?) Good golly Miss Molly what folly!

Anyway at that time, President Bush with his New World Order shit rained tons of missles up Saddam's assassanasious-lollycom and it didn't phase him.

Psychics, astrologers, seers, soothsayers, mediums 'n' readers, the world over at that time were scratchin' their heads 'n' other parts, tryin' to find a solution to that troublin' Gulf war dilemma to no avail. I recall quite clearly at that time, New York Daily News Astrologer, Joyce Jillson, misread the stars 'n' heavenly bodies when she predicted Saddam Hussein would commit suicide in December of 1990. It's suffice'nt to say, that's one prediction that bit the dust.

Astrology expert Joan Quigley, former first lady Nancy Reagen's personal astrologer, burnt the midnight oil, pouring over celestial charts 'n' plottin' the course of the stars to no avail, tryin' to find the answer to that perplexing dilemma, only to discover that the stars were movin' in Saddam's favor. Even Athena Starwoman, star gazer for Vogue, was vague in her visions, which weren't too vivid regarding that matter at that time.

Any fool will tell you, Saddam Hussein, a Taurus, born April 28, 1937, with Jupiter crossin' the ascendant with Pluto risin' three miles east of Venus, if you take the Freeway and arrive before the stars leave the Seventh House catchin' a brother as he leaves his house on his way to work up at the 'big house', passin' Rev. Jessie Jackson on his way from the outhouse to the White House. From this, you should be able to gather that a fool was loose in the desert, that should have been in the nut house. So wake up 'n' get a grip, befo' you end up in the po'house. My point is: if the psychics knew so much, why is Saddam Hussein still runnin' loose, causin' world leaders to quake in their boots?

Keep in mind, yo' cash ain't nothin' but trash to some people and they will gladly take it off of yo' hands. I'll say it again: Don't buy the hype, the melon may not be ripe, so thump it to make sure. In the past few years, so called psychics have been comin' out of the woodwork like worms wormin' their way into the pocketbooks 'n' check books of gullible nonthinkin' folks who want something for nothing, or refuse to use their God-given ability to think for themselves.

I can remember when White folks made light of Black psychics 'n' such, sayin' that it was superstition and the work of ungodly heathens, bereft of civility. This is a perfect example of blatant hypocrisy and scrapperlonious muddledge. Look at who the card shufflers, psychics, and astrologers are naw. Today's celebrity (hot house) mantologists, who claim to be 'gifted' in the arts of astrography 'n' cataphonics, are accepted with open arms 'n' pocketbooks. They have run Black seers 'n' psychics of yesteryear, whose arts were learned in the deep South, out of business. Because they are unable to compete with their hi-tech celebrity counterparts with their 900 numbers, TV infomercials and full-page ads in the supermarket tabloids. Back in the day, a foreteller or what not, could restore a man's nature or take it away from him and could mix up a batch of devil shoe string 'n' high John the conqueror root that would cure anything. I don't understand this mess today!

Not long ago, a well known Black actor/psychic, by the name of Billy Dee Williams, went up side his woman's head. Why didn't his kno' it all' psychic cohorts tell him that that wasn't cool, or better still why didn't he see it comin' 'n' restrain himself? Do you see where I'm goin' with this?

Ha, ha, ha, ha—what was her name? Come on you kno' who I'm talkin' 'bout. The Italian stallion's momma—Jackie, Jackie Stallone. Remember her? "I'm the worlds greatest astrologer. Do you want to hit the lotto? Call me! I can bring you love, happiness, success, money." Where is she now? Last I heard, she was four hundred thousand dollars in debt. How could that be? If she had a workin' relationship with the stars 'n' heavenly host, why didn't she prevail upon them to intercede in her behalf?

This is a dolorous (check it out) case to say the least. Michael Jackson's bemused sister LaToya, who married that crazy White man, has a psychic line you can avail yourself of and she and her psychics will advise you on the issues of life. If this ain't the most lamentable squittle-squattage I have ever heard of in my life, and in my time I have heard of some grievous shit. This poor deluded child has let that snake wrap itself aroun' her neck too long, too tight, cuttin' off much needed oxygen to her brain. It causes one to wonder, at what point in her petal-plucked life did she become endowed with powers of a fatiloquent (oh, you know what it means) nature? If she possesses the "gift" of psychic insight, why doesn't she heal her sick husband and her dysfunctional family, get herself out of debt and straighten out her moonstruck, moonwalkin' brother, Michael. This confused child couldn't see her way out of a paper bag, even if it had two holes for seein'.

This is the queen of them all: "Do You Know the Way To San Jose?" You all know who I'm talkin' about—Miss Dionne, first lady of the Psychic Friends Network. "Real help, genuine support and expert guidance are only a phone call away. All you need is a phone and an open mind." The Psychic Friends forget to mention that you will also need an open wallet, checkbook, or valid credit card. And another thing, why didn't they (the Psychic Friends) tell Wolfman Jack that he was goin' to drop dead from a heart attack? Perhaps the stars were sort of dim that fateful day. If these people are the dispensers of help and guidance, why do they use the disclaimer "For adults and entertainment purposes only?"

However, scores of gullible people flock to these false psychics 'n' what not. As a word to the wise, the spirit worlds are not to be played with or taken lightly. It certainly is not a playground! I was taken aback when I saw J.J.'s momma Florida (Good Times) on TV peddling psychic advice—"Tell them Ester (Rolle) sent you." Umph.....

This is a lulu—The First Lady (Hillary Clinton) is not the only one communin' with the dead people. A psychic/medium by the name of Andre

Talivere said that he was able to call upon The Great Soul of Ghandi during a seance and these predictions were revealed: The 21st Century will be the (some of you women are goin' to like this!) beginning of the era of the woman. In the marriage contract, the man will agree to total subservience (some are already doin' it!) to his wife. No marriage contract can be terminated by the man, but must be ended by the woman. It will be a period of harmonious relations between man and woman—a return to old values (when the man treated the woman with a heavy hand?) with a new conscience. Umph, umph, umph!!! Brood upon this one! Wake up people. Think! Psychic my Aunt Fanny.....

Don't buy the hype. I once witnessed a truck carryin' a load of sugar up the street and the flies followed it. A truck load of stinkin' garbage came down the street. The flies left the sugar truck 'n' followed the garbage truck. Some people are like flies, they will jump on any truck that happens to pass by!

# STRESS!!!

*L*ook aroun' you and you will see things today that's not fit to see. Hear things that's not fit to hear and see people doin' things that's not fit to do, in turn, causin' stress. Yesterday I saw a skinny woman who looked like she was ready for the undertaker, stealin' flowers from a hearse. I said, "Miss you should be ashamed of yo' se'f, stealin' flowers from the dead!" She said, "I gots to git mines, the man in the casket can't smell 'em, so I'm goin' to sell 'em."

The mourners watched stunned as she fashioned bouquets, yellow on the outside white in the middle, 'n' sold them to people visiting the sick in the hospital.

A young boy tried to hold me up last week. He said, "Yo pops, do you kno' what time it is?" I said, "If you want to kno' the time, go to work 'n' buy yo'se'f a watch." "You are my employer," he said 'n' broke bad, compellin' me to reach into my bag 'n' take out my 'check book' 'n' write him a check...BANG!!! He hauled ass howlin' in pain. As he hobbled to the hospital to get it cashed, I hurried to put my smokin' check book away before the police came, because I didn't have a license, ha, ha, ha....

You're afraid to walk the street naw days. Take the case of hip-hop Harold a hip-hoppin' hom' boy from Harlem who was charged with assault 'n' battery for inflictin' grave bodily harm upon Herman Hampton of Harmon with a hand gun in broad daylight' in the presence of six cops, four nuns, 'n' a priest. Hip Harold swore that he didn't do it. He insisted that Mr. Hampton inflicted the injuries upon himself when he ran into the bullet even though he (Hip Harold) was holdin' the smokin' gun.

Harvey Hudson, a hardened lawyer from Hoboken, was appointed to defend hip-hoppin' Harold before judge Helen Haley using the 'black rage' defense, but Judge Haley wasn't hardly about to sit still for it. She tongue lashed Hip Harold's attorney. "You must think that I'm crazy, fiddle-funked 'n' fuckedupas Colin Ferguson, the Long Island Rail Road gunman. Even he didn't buy into that convoluted defense, neither will I," said the judge, as she sent hip-hop Harold up the river, for life plus thirty days. But the judge's sentence didn't please Herman Hampton. He rose from his wheel-chair 'n' exacted his own retribution upon hip-hop Harold, with a .38. Umph!

We live in a society that creates it's own problems, due to its members thinkin' 'n' actions; then we spend time and money studying them, when the problem is plain as your nose in your face. I've come to this conclusion, because it is the only conclusion in my opinion to come to, so I concluded: When a study is done on somethin'—lookout! Here comes another study to study the original study that was studied incorrectly in the first place. The so called experts, it seems to me, spend their every wakin' moment tryin' to decide what they will study next.

This is a lulu: A few years ago, The National Science Foundation concluded a study to study the sex life of the Lane County, Oregon, salamander. The study revealed that "observing the reproductive behavior in salamanders presents tremendous methodological problems, owing to the cryptic or nocturnal behavior of most salamanders." What do you make of this goobly-gook? Keep in mind these people are highly paid with your tax money for this kind of nonsense. Who in hell cares about screwin' salamanders?

According to a recent study, stress is on the rise 'n' the experts are tryin' to determine why people are so stressed out. They should ask me, I could tell 'em: Complex livin' conditions, lies, and distortions that people have allowed to be perpetrated upon them over a long period of time, is what's causin' them to 'bug out', 'go wack', and in extreme cases, like Congressman Dogooder's wife, have to be committed to an institution for the moonstruck, all because they listen to and allow any and everyone to lead them down the garden path, only to find out that there are no vegetables growin'. Like mad people, they chase the nightmare called, the "American Dream", which will stress a saint.

In today's rabidly materialistic climate, people are becomin' consumer addicts. They purchase fast, expensive automobiles, then have to leave them parked on the street, because they can't find or afford to rent space in a garage, then worry all night, hoping that it will be where they parked it when they awaken after havin' taken a sleepin' pill to get a good night's sleep in that house, apartment, co-op, or condo that they are struggling to pay the rent or mortgage on. They jump up 'n' jet to that stressful job that they despise 'n' pray that they can get back home without being highjacked, car jacked, sky jacked, or jacked up. They're constantly being bugged, bombarded 'n' bothered by beggars, braggers, peddlers 'n' meddlers. It amazes me 'n' I don't amaze easily, because I have seen it all and if there's anything left to see, I don't want to see it!

My ass has been set on fire, lit by my own hand, leavin' me three cents short of a dollar, which don't go too far these days. Today's compulsive consumer has armed himself with every credit card known to man and alien. They will charge everything that is in fashion or has a designer label on it and is out of style before they can get it out of the store or falls apart shortly thereafter, while they are still payin' for it.

There are those who become so besides themselves, as it were, with greed 'n' grabbin' in search of an easier way to fame 'n' fortune that they lie, cheat, steal, and in some cases, stay up until the wee hours of the night, placing orders for junk that is offered up on the Home Shoppers Network, that they have never heard of, have no need for, but purchase anyway, in order that they will have something else that they are unable to pay for as they run head long into bankruptcy, join debtors anonymous or sink into drugs 'n' alcohol abuse, and in extreme cases become moonstruck and have to seek help from a psychiatrist, which won't do them much good, because the psychiatrist from whom they are seeking help is seeking help from a psychiatrist for his or her own mental and emotional aberrations and are six sessions short of a cure themselves. It's a sad 'n' sorry sight to see a poor soul in the grip of the consumption monster. They become bereft of reason. You all know that The Sweetman is tellin' the truth. Right now, even as I speak, som' of you are payin' for Christmas presents that you purchased last year on your credit card. This kind of pressure, coupled with the fear of loss of employment, escalatin' taxes, down sizin', lay-offs, price hikes, and crime, is enough to stress a gorilla and drive it out of its mind, ha, ha, ha,...umph, shut yo' mouf! Here is another stress factor that will put a bee in yo' bonnet 'n' a burr up yo', oh well, anyway, oh boy!

This is a mess. Look out, here com' stress: Boy meets girl, girl meets girl, boy meets boy, man meets beast—oops, I'm not gonna go there. In these days of political correctness, I don't want to leave out anyone—anyway, two people meet, they have eyes for each other and their noses are opened up so wide, a Mack truck could be driven up it. They are 'in love'. Umph!

These young love bugs' hormones start hummin' 'n' short circuit their brains, causin' them to take leave of their common sense, thus rendering them bereft of reason. They run aroun' like a chicken with its head cut off, tellin' everyone who will stand still and listen to them, "I'm in love." Well I'm here to tell you, you are insane! Muttlestruck! No sound foundation has been laid for real lastin' love. What's up wit dat? Since the beginnin' of time, raw passion-laden romantic relationships have driven many men and women to wax maniacal. In their entwinement of love, they cry "I'm so in love, I can't live without you", "I've never loved anyone, the way I love you", "I can' live without you", "If you leave me I will kill myself","If I can't have you, no one else will." These are a few of the utterances that slide from betwixt the lips of those in the grip of extreme romantic emotion, which has caused the most pestiferous sufferin' to those who fall victim to this emotionally unsound erotic affliction. What goes wrong in these tragic cases? Let's take a look!

This case takes the cake 'n' a few fruitloops: A 'brother' by the name of Othello, the Moor, became moon-dusted for Desdemona, a young lady of alabaster hue. When they first hooked-up, it was, "Oh Desdemona, how I love thee." That was of course before a White boy by the name of Iago, put shit in the game, causin' bro Othello to lapse into epileptic-like fits, 'n' be thrown into a broodin' state of pathos, which drove him to enter their bed chamber, where Desdemona was asleep. Sweatin' profusely, eyes bulgin', Othello 'roused Desdemona from her slumber 'n' inquired, "Desdemona, has thou prayed tonight?" Before she could open her mouth to answer his strange inquiry, "Strumpet," he bellowed 'n' commenced to choke the wind out of her. "Oh Desdemona I do love thee I do love thee," he said. "Then why choketh me and call me 'ho', my Lord," she thought to herself, as she struggled for air.

After Othello choked Desdemona to death, he stood up 'n' started talkin' crazy shit 'bout a dog that was runnin' loose uncircumcised, then he plunged a knife into himself 'n' crawled on top of her 'n' expired. Have you ever heard of such shit? I kno' it causes a rumblin' betwixt my lower quarters. In my unlettered opinion, in the case of some lovers, cupid dips his or her arrow of love into the poison vat of obsession 'n' sends it flyin' into unstable hearts, sendin' them into the abyss of hugger-mugger.

What these young (or old, 'n' that's worse) eager love beavers don't understand is fallin' in love is sex-linked and erotic in nature, is temporary at best, and soon fades like moon flowers come day break, or morning glories come night fall. They rush head long 'n' shack up. "We want to get to know each other," they say. They already "know" each other, probably "knew" one another on the day or night they met. How much more knowin' do they need? Well, anyway, they move in together, break up, make up, get married, divorced, then start the whole dysfunctional process over again.

As the years go by they go through lovers and one night stands like crazed locusts through a field of grain, leavin' in its wake hurt, confused off-spring, resentment and sometimes even murder.

Frank Sinatra recorded a song years ago. I kno' you have heard it. *Love and marriage, love and marriage, go together like a horse and carriage...* These days folks get hitched 'n' unhitched befo' the ink is dry on the marriage certificate. The horse go in one direction and the carriage in another, as they look for someone else to get hitched up with. All this hitchin' 'n' unhitchin' is enough to stress a horse 'n' make a mule throw up its tail 'n' holler, "I can't take it!"

Holidays when families get together can cause stress to run amuck 'n' cause ruckus 'n' ruin during these festive occasions. I've known blows to be struck 'n' fire power to be unleashed, causin' grave consequences. Durin' these festive occasions, built up resentments, anger, and hostility are unleashed at the dinner table as the turkey is being carved. Case in point: On Thanksgiving day 1995, a father 'n' daughter in Queens (New York) got into a heated embroilment at the dinner table. The child grabbed a gun 'n' shot her daddy as he was about to bite into a turkey leg, causin' him to finish his dinner elsewhere. Right here in Harlem, one Christmas day a boy got into a' ugly embranglement with his momma 'n' slapped a slice of ham outa her mouth, because she had him circumcised when he was a baby without his consent.

I have witnessed a number of these explosive outbursts, right after grace was said. On holidays, there is always one family member who will ruin the festivities, causin' others in the family to scramble to the medicine cabinet for something to calm their nerves.

It usually goes something like this: A chill is in the air, autumn leaves fallin' gently to the ground. Winter is not far away, tomorrow is Thanksgiving day. Pies in the oven bakin'. Mashed potatoes, turnips, candied yams in heavy syrup of brown sugar, butter, allspice, cinnamon, collard greens with smoked ham hocks cookin', as mom prepares cranberry sauce, roast pork, ham glazed with pineapple, turkey roasted to perfection, stuffed with mom's stuffin'. No better stuffin' was ever stuffed into a turkey. Giblet gravy, rich 'n' brown, the aroma can be smelled all over town.

The table is set. Candles lit. Glasses, plates, silver in place. Everyone is seated. "Grandpa, will you please say grace?" "Lord, we thank you for this food. Bless those who have less in da' hood. Those who are homeless, naked, hungry, house, clothe 'n' feed. Lord this is all I got to say. Thank you for another Thanksgiving day. Amen!"

The dinner is over. Everyone is stuffed with stuffin', the whole family was pleased with the greeze. Grandpa is in his easy chair, coppin' some zzzz's. Aunt Mable is the only one left at the table, sippin' on her fifth glass of wine. The family begins to get uneasy. Aunt Mable stands up, her wig falls off. She puts her hands on her hips. What jive will come from her lips? Her speech is slurred 'n' slow. She brought up some jive that happened thirty years ago. "You 'member when you, blah, blah, blah." You get the picture? Can you identify?

Because you didn't listen to the Sweetman, you bought the hype, when you cut it open, the melon wasn't ripe 'n' you find yourself trapped, like those rats greasy Pete trapped, skinned, cooked, then sold to you, as he scratched his ass, pissed, and didn't wash his hands because he knew you would buy and eat anything that look like it is barbecued. Good Lord, people whutup wit dat? Get a grip!

In this youth oriented culture, there are those who will allow so-called fitness gurus, beauty, youth, fashion, and health experts, through the power of the mass media, who can make a dead serpent look appealin''n' a' alligator look tame. These merchants of snake oil can make you feel useless, stupid, dumb, old, ugly, 'n' fat if you don't subscribe to or purchase their courses, schemes, teaching, diets, creams, lotions, 'n' potions, which is supposed to make you feel and look younger, sexier, thinner, 'n' trimmer.

The slick talkin' dream peddlers, through their infomercials, 900 numbers, TV, radio, and print ads, for a good portion of your hard earned money promise to show you how to buy a house with no money down. If this be true, may I be so bold as to ask "How come there are so many homeless people sleepin' on the street, in stations of public conveyance, on park benches, over hot air grates, in subway trains, and under cardboard boxes?

The market is flooded with books, courses, tapes, and videos that are supposed to fulfill your dreams of fame 'n' fortune. Umph! Remember this: Waitin' in the wings are highly paid social researchers (with taxpayers' money) standin' by to study you and your wacked out behavior to ascertain why you are goin' bananas. Wake up! Before you crack up! The bottom line is, you are paying to drive yourself crazy, nutty, gim-crack, 'n' what not! This is a mess.

Consider, if you will, when a consumer is in the grip of compulsion, showin' him or her a new fangled what-you-ma'-call-it, or gizmo, is like danglin' a fried chicken in front of a preacher, a vote or contribution in front of a politician, a vial of crack in front of a crackhead, a dish of Tender Vittles in front of a feline, or food of any kind, in front of Marlon Brando, who had to be fork lifted on the set of CNN's "Larry King Live", where his lips flew open 'n' googobs of ill-chosen verbiage flew from betwixt his teeth, regardin' so called Jewish influence (don't buy the hype) in Hollywood and their lack of sensitivity when portrayin' African-Americans, Orientals, Indians, 'n' etc., etc. in films. If I may be so bold as to inquire: "Why didn't he protest the dialogue in "Godfather I"—the line that went: "Send the drugs up to Harlem, niggers are nothing but animals anyway," or words to that effect. Did this revelation suddenly dawn upon him? I think not. Well, anyway it caused the Jewish community mo' stress 'n' outrage than Professor Leonard Jeffries, former head of the Black Studies Department at City University of New York. Loose lips sink ships, start wars, 'n' ass kickin', 'n' stress. Some people like to stir up shit for their own narrow purposes. Folks say to me, "Sweetman, you are outspoken." I don't think that I have to tell you again what you can do if you don't like what I say.

Slick talkin' teachers, activists, gurus, 'n' what not will take yo' mind 'n' money 'n' leave you broke, dumb, and out in the cold. Beware! I, The Sweetman, don't need what they're sellin' 'n' damn sho' ain't gullible enough to believe what they're sayin'. So they can kiss my—wait a minute, I ain't goin' to invite nobody way up yonder, it ain't nice. Let me shut my mouf, my lips are gittin' loose. I got to practice what I preach befo' I cause stress, mess 'n' duress...ha, ha, ha...Umph! Oh my goodness.

Sex, sex, sex, umph, urnph, umph! This is a hot topic that will melt ice at the North Pole 'n' cause a polar bear to sweat. Sex is a subject that has been studied, restudied, hashed 'n' re-hashed, hushed up, shied away from, swept under the rug, 'n' whispered about in the dark since the day Adam sank his choppers into that apple and became aware that Eve was naked.

**SEX!**

*U*ntil recent times, sex was performed in the dark. Now days, however, it's done anytime, anywhere, even in broad day light. Umph! After tens of thousands of years, man is still studyin' sex tryin' to figure out how to do it, when to do it, and the right and wrong ways to do it. Every sexpert from Dr. Freud to Dr. Ruth—a short sweet little Jewish woman who looks like she should be at home (I'm skatin' on thin ice) in the kitchen makin' chicken soup and who is America's leadin' sexpert, who counsels 'n' gives sexual sage to the sexually confused, on how to do it, who to do it with, or to, and if you have no one to do it with, do it to yourself and experience self satisfaction, given the fact that often times doin' it with someone else can prove to be unsatisfactory. Whew!

That was a mouthful, no pun intended. Let us examine the various sexual classifications: heterosexual, bisexual, homosexual. Let The Sweetman clarify this for you. It is my belief that with a simplification of the matter under discussion, it will allow you to recognize, therefore, causin' you no further befuddlement. Simply. A heterosexual is one who has heard 'bout sex, but never had any. A bisexual is one who let sex pass them by, in other words, they can take it or leave it. However, when they do, they take it from both directions. Umph! A homosexual on the other hand—now, that's another matter (let me be delicate, I don't want to start no mess). A homosexual is a person who has sex at home and a few other places the park...ha, ha, ha, ha. Umph! Let me pull myself together, fo' I go too far afield.

On a serious tip, sex is used to lure, hook, snare, snookle, and sell everything from girl scout cookies to pots 'n' pans. Sex has driven some men and women to inflict grave bodily harm upon one another, and in extreme cases, commit *coup de grace*. Umph! I have seen men in the throes of carnality, ask for, beg, buy, and in extreme cases, wax rapacious and forcefully help themselves against the woman's will.

A beast who does this should be shot. As a consequence of this ubiquitous sexual climate in which we find ourselves today, which, I may add, is hotter than a steamy Georgia swamp in the summertime, sexually transmitted diseases are rampant, wreakin' havoc, puttin' a strain on the health care system. In spite of this, the powerful urge for concupiscent indulgence drives some men, women, 'n' young folk to run headlong with wanton determination in their zealous pursuit of carnality and lickerish gratification, sending them into a state of sexual hugger-mugger.

The calm of the midnight hour is wrenched asunder by the moanin' 'n' groanin', yowlin' 'n' howlin' of the rankest and most goatish nature, which can be heard in the White House, State House, 'ho' house, bath house, road house, hen house, 'n' every other house.

In the bed room, bath room, board room, on the dance floor, in cars, on the highways, byways, in doorways, alleyways, 'n' every which-a-way, from under every bush, shrub and tree in the park...Umph! Excuse me while I wipe the sweat from my brow. Other than fire, this subject causes me to perspire.

Sex is a billion dollar business: movies, 900 sex lines, magazines, peep shows, top 'n' bottomless bars, records, videos, radio, television, talk shows, cable, and now On Line 'n' Cyberspace, are breedin' grounds and outlets for every sexual proclivity imaginable, and in too many instances, young children have unrestrained access to these lubricious venues. No wonder teen-aged pregnancy is on the rise.

Case in point: Out in Lusthaven, a pimpley faced boy by the name of Peter Perkins, who was watchin' an adult film on cable TV while his parents were out for the evening, was thrown prematurely into puberty. He started to feel perky, and with pecker raised, he ran forth with lurid intent and hit on winsome Wendy Wilson, a wasp-waisted waif of a girl.

The boy's concupiscent hunger was of such a salacious nature, that upon findin' Wendy, the boy wailed, whined, whimpered, begged 'n' went wack. He fell upon his knees before Wendy. "What are you doing, Peter Perkins?" asked Wendy. "Praying, giving thanks for what I'm about to receive," said Peter. Before Wendy could catch wind of what Peter was up to, with clumsy effort, Peter removed the obstruction that stood between him 'n' his impendin' pleasure. Like a wild wart hog eatin' walnuts in Warsaw, Peter dined ruttishely upon Wendy's barely developed fur burger. Suddenly Wendy uttered a loud cry that pierced the night. "P-e-e-e-t-e-r," Wendy wailed. She grabbed Peter by the collar of his shirt 'n' screamed, "Get up!" Peter jumped up 'n' Wendy Wilson went down befo' Peter and "helped" herself to Peter like Peter helped himself to her. Then Peter, (done what he had seen on cable) laid Wendy upon the earth, she threw her limbs asunder, hurriedly. Peter crawled betwixt her quarters, and they "knew" each other with wanton intensity.

Upon returnin' home Peter was flushed 'n' grinnin' like a cat that had just swallowed a canary. Peter's mother Pauline Perkins remarked, "Oh dear! How amazing. I had no idea that pimple cream I purchased for you yesterday would clear up your complexion so quickly!"

Meanwhile, over at Wendy's house, Wendy's mom, Wanda Wilson said to her daughter, "Sweetheart why look at your chest. Mommy's little girl has blossomed over night." Deflowered is more like it. Umph! Umph! Umph!

So you may ask: "What is the solution to this sexual situation?" Sweetman will tell you. In today's nymphomaniacal society, sex education is of the utmost necessity. Therefore, parents must not be perfunctory in their parental duty or wax pusillanimous when discussing blossomhood with their pubescent youth. Sit down and explain to them why the salmon are swimming upstream, and how, when, and what hour of the day or night the stork will appear. When a child's privates become private and they enter the stage of juvenilia, their hormones leave the lower regions and move to the upper room. This ain't no jive, when bees start swaying around the flowers, they're going to make honey in the hive.

A pubescent male child in the throes of juvenilia approaching a young girl's garden bearing two full sacks of fertilizer will not have gardening on his mind. Therefore, mothers must instruct their adolescent daughters in the art of keeping their garden gate closed, and fathers their sons how to keep their fertilizer in storage until the fertile soil of the marriage bed is ready. When sap starts rising in the tree, maple syrup won't be far behind.

During juvenescence, an adolescent will dwell upon the opposite sex with intense affection, except for those rare few whose hormones take a left turn in the other direction. Whew!

This phase of life can also prove embarrassing: Johnny standing before the class erecting a science project suddenly gets a spontaneous erection. Embarrassed, he hurries from the class room and horn-harks his drabbus in the boys room at recess. At this point, an understanding adult should explain to the youth what is occurring. The child doesn't need to hear no foolishness about go get his eyes checked because he's going blind. Tell the children the truth. Parents, if you don't take the responsibility for your children's sex education, someone else will.

Do you remember a few years back, when a few so-called sexperts in the educational system of New York City came up with the "Cucumber curriculum?" If those so called sexperts would have had their way, the class room would have looked like a porno fruit stand. These people wanted to demonstrate the proper way to put on a condom by using a cucumber, banana, or some other elongated vegetable, such as a zucchini. Bananas belong in a banana split, zucchinis are usually eaten raw, sautéed, steamed, baked or made into a bread, and cucumbers are used in salads, mixed with sour cream or pickled. If saner minds had not prevailed, there's no tellin' what kind of ruttish notions these fruit 'n' vegetables would have stirred up in young impressionable minds.

If this mess had not been checked, young people would have most likely become mixed up (more than they are) like a fruit salad and perhaps would have acted out on their scrappinacious feelin's of a goatish nature, causin' some to wax lickerish and grabbinate their drabbus with a cucumber in the privacy of their room or scuddlate a banana in the bathroom and zapperlone a zucchini with a friend after school.

Would some teachers have lost control (many have) and waxed horsennacious in the presence of those fresh fruits 'n' vegetables? Perhaps others would have taken leave of their facilities and hummbulate their tittleledge with a student in the faculty lounge at recess.

It amazes me, that some of today's teachers are unable to teach students the three R's, but they can teach them how to horn-hark their drabbus with a cucumber.

Because of this rampant sexual atmosphere, teen-aged pregnancy is on the rise, which gives rise to another problem. Abortion. This bein' a very sensitive issue, I will proceed with the greatest delicacy and caution, taking into account the amount of emotion this subject evokes in some folks. Some say that you should, others say you shouldn't, some say they would, others couldn't, due to moral and religious considerations. The scriptures say, "Be fruitful and multiply." However, parents must impress upon their offspring that, if they are too young, or not ready to bear fruit and the responsibility of fruit rearing, they must delay depositing or allowing any seeds to be deposited in the fertile feminine soil, which could sprout and produce a flower which they may be forced to pluck up prematurely in the short run, causing them to regret it in the long run.

Let me now for the moment address all the young men present here tonight. So listen up. It's time for all of you to take responsibility for your actions. Before you engage in the act of swinery, go in the drug sto', buy yo' self a condominium and put it on yo' gentile. An' you young ladies mak' sho' that he do it, 'cause he's goin' to protest "I don' wan' to put on no condiminium, 'cause it don' feel right." Girl, you grab a hold of his fornicative instrument, snake yo' neck, 'n' say, 'Now you looka here Mr. Goodstuff, if you don't wear a condominium, I will not let you com' in the penthouse, 'cause I kno' damned well you ain't goin' to pay the rent if you give me a full house. If you ain't ready to do the right thing, git to steppin.'" (Now you go girl, that's tellin' 'em.) Remember, if you play post office, expect to deliver some mail.

Today's inflamed sexual situation is out of hand, causin' every Tom, Dick 'n' Henrietta to come out of the woodwork with crazy solutions. Case in point: Hillary Rodham Clinton, Bill's wife, was in a deep funk in the White House kitchen whippin' up a batch of cookies, broodin' over the fact that her much touted health care plan had collapsed, and all the cattle had run off and there was no future(s) left in that so she found herself up the 'Whitewater' river without a paddle, where the Republicans are still fishin'. It will be interesting to see what they catch.

Suddenly, BANG! A brilliant idea dawned upon Hillary. She took off her apron and rushed over to Oprah Winfrey's house. Frantically she rang the door bell, ding-a-ling, ding-a-ling, ding-a-ling. "Who is it?" Oprah asked, annoyed. "It's me, Hillary." Oprah opened the door, "Come..." before she could get another word out of her mouth, Hillary rushed in, almost knockin' her down. Oprah jumped back. "Hillary! What's the matter?" Oprah inquired. Hillary flopped down into an easy chair, threw her hands up, and exclaimed "Oprah, Oprah, Oprah! I have the most revolutionary idea. Quick! Turn on the cameras, I want to announce it to the world! Oprah stood in the floor taken-a-back. She cast her eyes heavenward, shrugged her shoulders, threw up her hands and said, "OK! Roll cameras."

Hillary, lookin' grave, gazed into the camera and said, "Hello, I'm Hillary Rodham Clinton (as if we didn't kno'), Bill's wife. I spoke with Mrs. Eleanor Roosevelt and had the most extraordinary revelation! I am happy to announce that I have found the solution to teenaged sexuality and pregnancy." Snatching (recycling) the words right out of Nancy Reagan's mouth—"Just Say No!" said Hillary with great satisfaction.

Ain't this a kick in the hind quarters? How can she give advice on sex, of all subjects, when her spouse was cultivating the flowers in Jennifer

Flowers' flower bed, when he should have been home, pickin' the peas in her pea patch. Can you imagine what young people think when they hear and see the things that older people say 'n' do?

Fathers, or some adult male (if you can find one), should instruct their sons that callin' women 'ho's is improper. When you hear young boys goin' 'roun' sayin' ho, ho, ho. Look where they got it from: Santa Claus, that's who! Roun' Christmas time there are hundreds of Santas on the street going, "Ho, ho, ho!" Christmas last I saw Santa ringin' his bell 'n' goin', "Ho, ho, ho," and some women turned 'roun', thinkin' he was talkin' to them...ooops.

# WHO CAN YOU TRUST?

Who can you trust these days? Your lawyer, doctor, dentist, rabbi, minister, priest, preacher, family, friend, or teacher? I'll tell you who you can trust:The Sweetman, that's who. You all kno' that. Like Moms Mabley, I tell you the truth. But do you listen to me? Oh, no! You rather listen to the fast talkers, con artists, crooks, 'n' charlatans, who make you believe that they can make you rich over night without workin', or tell you how they can take your life savings and triple it by daybreak, makin' you rich. With your eyes closed, ears stopped up, pocket book and check book wide open, you buy what these charlatans are peddlin', even crazy shit like: They (the crooks) can turn a' eighty year old person into a teenager, and defy death. While you are bein' fooled 'n' fleeced, you drop dead, and the con man's lips are still movin' faster than Amtrak as he picks your pockets while you lay stiff as a board. Wake-up!

These fast-talkin' flim-flammin' fleecers can talk a bone out of a pit bull's mouth, scales off of a fish, the shirt or skirt off of your back, 'n' look at you with a straight face 'n' make you believe that you are fully clothed as they hold your garments in their hands, while you stand naked as a jay bird with yo' ass freezin' off. Ain't this four brazen bitches at the branch with their tails waggin'? Umph!

Durin' the course of your life, like O.J. Simpson, you find yourself in need of the services of a liar—oops! I mean lawyer or Dream Team. If that need should arise, I beg of you to heed the Sweetman's advice: Exercise due caution! I say this because slick talkin' barristers 'n' "fast food" type law firms are springin' up like crazed mushrooms. They (the lawyers) will snatch your money, misrepresent you, then stash their ill-gotten gains offshore or in Swiss banks. While they have fun, frolic, 'n' sun themselves on the French Riviera, you 'n' your family collect soda cans and struggle to make ends meet in your new home (a cardboard box) down by the Amtrak tracks. In the spirit of fairness however, let me make this perfectly clear (where have I heard that one?). Not all lawyers are crooks. There are those who are honest (ha, ha, ha....oops!), but be aware of those who will think nothing of strippin' you of house 'n' home or country!

Case in point: The New York Times reported a few years ago that a greedy, grabbin', money grubbin' group of gyp artist and scheming lawyers colluded with an avaricious gang of double-dealing investment bankers and assorted Wall Street crooks to defraud a tiny country the size of a turnip patch (population 10,000). This one is for the birds. It was birds dung that made the people of this small Pacific Island of Nauru, located just below the equator, wealthy. Nauru's massive reserves of fossilized ancient bird droppings which are rich in phosphate and which is used in the manufacturing of fertilizer, created a boomin' business for this small republic.

Unfortunately, the phosphate rich bird shit reserves were running out, because after years of plundering by the Germans in 1886 and two centuries of colonization, it would be entirely depleted within a few years.

Upon observing which-a-way the islands financial winds were blowin', the officials of the republic of Nauru became alarmed and decided the prudent thing to do was to invest—but in what? The officials of Nauru approached one Ronald Powles, an Australian attorney, who persuaded them to invest twenty-nine million dollars in a bogus financial instrument called, "Standby letters of credit." Standby indeed! Stand by 'n' be fleeced.

Well anyway, Ronald Powles, along with a gaggle of crooked U.S.A. lawyers, bankers and brokers, acted in collusion and commenced to fleece the Island of Nauru faster than a snowball melts in hell. Take it from me, that's quick. The Naaruns, seeing that the winds of financial growth were not blowing in their direction, and recalling how the Germans and others had fleeced them of their precious bird manure, were not about to stand still like sheep 'n' be fleeced by this gaggle of crooks, who were caught with their stealing drawers down and dealt with to the fullest extent of the law. Good. Ain't this a' ugly mess? You can't trust no one with shit these days, bird or otherwise. What's goin' on? Check this out.

According to a recent study, alcoholism and drug addiction among today's young lawyers are on the rise. They are unable to pass the bar, pass a bar, without going in, getting bombed, and acting like bums, thus affecting their ability to defend their clients, some of whom are being fleeced faster than Jim Bakker fleeced his flock.

They'll go along with scrappinacious abolum presented by the prosecution, object to their own objection, and rule on their own motion. These young legal eagles are stressed out, strung out, and will bug out before the judge and jury, thinking that jurisprudence is a drink and *corpus delicti,* a dessert.

Some lawyers become unruly, and won't wait for the judge to rule. They jump the gun and overrule themselves. They'd confuse the haggar hippist with the *habaes corpus* and don't know the difference. They don't know how to write a brief, are too brief or not brief enough, or some of them forget to put the brief in their briefcase. A young lawyer stood before the judge without his briefs. He was robbed of his clothes on his way to court. Since he wasn't wearing briefs, it caused a brief commotion. The judge called for a brief recess.

This is an interesting case: Barrister Barbara Burrell of Burlington was defending Babs Babcock, a batted hooker, charged with assault and battery for beating her pimp, Big Black Bernie, with a baseball bat. Barrister Barbara Burrell took hooker Babs Babcock's bread and split with Big Black Bernie the pimp to Bermuda, leaving hooker Babs Babcock defenseless at the bar broke, holding the bag.

Upon her release from jail, Babs Babcock caught up with Barrister Barbara Burrell and Big Black Bernie in Boston. The two women fought. Babs Babcock beat Barrister Barbara Burrell so bad her store-bought braids fell off of her head and left her bald. Big Black Bernie beat Babs Babcock for beating him with the baseball bat. They kissed and made up and bald headed Barrister Barbara Burrell was disbarred.

In today's sue happy environment, the country is overrun with fast-food types of law firms who will sue a can of Raid for killin' a roach. These fast talkin' sue-happy barristers will file a lawsuit in your or my behalf at the drop of a legal pad. Even if you don't have a strong case, they will skitterlop the legal oberloumb 'n' make a case anyway. If you have an inklin' that you may be struck down by a baby carriage on your way to work, contact one of these flim-flam law firms before leavin' home and they will meet you at the accident scene and threaten the baby to settle out of court or face a court case. These ambulance chasers have been known to chase an ambulance to an accident scene and thrust their business cards into a dead man's hand—oops, oh shit, or woman's—and say, "Call me, we have a case." If these shysters can't find someone to sue, they sue each other. Doctors are scared to death of them.

Doctors. Umph! Last week I was feelin' kinda poorly, so I went to the doctor. I could just as well have stayed home. I said, "Doc, I don't feel well." He coughed in my face and said, "Neither do I." He wrote me a prescription. "What is this for Doc?" I asked. "It's for whatever ails you," he said, as he sat behind his desk, coughin' 'n' sneezin' 'n' poppin' pills. A man went to the doctor and said, "Doctor, doctor, help me, I feel like I'm dying." "Why come to me? Go to the undertaker," the doctor said. A woman went to the doctor because she was having trouble with her eyes. The doctor told her to undress. He commenced to examine her private members. "Doctor," the lady protested, "The pain is in my eyes. Why are you fumblin' around down there?" "When I look up this end, I can see better what's wrong with your eyes," the doctor answered. Ugly!!

A man went to the hospital to have a leg amputated. The doctor removed the good leg. Upon discovering his mistake, he said, "Oops," then removed the one that he was supposed to remove in the first place. When the man went to the hospital, he expected to leave on crutches. Instead he left in a wheelchair.

The average person goes to the doctor at least five times a year. The doctor vacations in Europe seven times a year. A woman went to the doctor to be artificially inseminated. The doctor was out of sperm, so he mounted her 'n' deposited his own. When he crawled off of her, he handed her a bill—a pimpin' doctor! Umph, umph, umph! Who can you trust? A White woman went to a New York sperm bank to be inseminated. Nine months later she gave birth to a Black baby. Surprise! Guess who's comin' to dinner! You ladies had better stay out of those sperm banks, because there's no tellin' what you will give birth to, because you don't know who's making deposits. I know of a woman who wanted to have a child without bein' wallowed on by a man—which is the way to go, that's my opinion. Anyway, two years later, in the throes of labor, she gave birth to "something" that jumped out of her, squawked 'n' flew out of the hospital window. Medical scientists, anthropologists, 'n' zoologists from all over the world are hoping to determine what it is, but they haven't been able to catch it. Who can you trust? Not the butcher, the baker, or the candlestick maker. Go the dentist to get a tooth pulled, you may wind up with somethin' in yo' mouth and it may not be a dental instrument.

Hold up, wait a minute. This is a Lulu Miss Sue. You would think that the one person you could trust would be your pastor, priest, rabbi, spiritual advisor, or what-not. Not necessarily so!

Take the case of vivacious Vicki Vaughan, the bereaved wife of Vinny Vaughan, a vicious villain who met an untimely demise. In her grief, widow Vicki sought comfort from her spiritual advisor, the Venerable Vernon Verrley, the Vicor of Vackershire, a small hamlet on the outskirts of London. After a brief prayer, Vicor Vernon Verrley got beside himself and flung his prayer book asunder. He then removed his vestments and voraciously engaged in an act of venery with the distraught Miss Vicki in the vestibule of the Vestry. Vicor Vernon Vealey's villainous violation of Miss Vicki brought disrepute upon the Vicarage. Umph, umph, umph!

Now you can see with all the mess that's goin' on in this world today, a little laughter is quite necessary. Ha, ha, ha...A hundred 'n' five year ol' man went to the 'ho' house. The madam asked, "Sir, why are you here at your age?" The old man said, "I want som' action." The madam said, "Sir, at your age, it's over." The old man said, "How much do I owe you?" Ha, ha! An oldie but a goody.

There's craziness everywhere. Even in heaven. One day the Lord was havin' trouble with White folks up in heaven. The White folks got uppity 'n' wouldn't wear their wings and refused to drink 'n' eat the sweet milk and honey. I can't blame them. Anyway, they pissed 'n' moaned 'n' carried on because they could not have steak 'n' baked potato with a green garden salad. The women didn't want to wear the long heavenly dresses and bras, they complained that their silicon bottoms were encumbered and the wings made them look like crazy birds. The men, who had wheeled 'n' dealed on earth, plotted to sell the Pearly Gates and streets of gold, 'n' sneak back to earth and make a fortune.

St. Peter saw what the White folks were up to so he went unto the Lord 'n' said, "Lord, I hate—I mean I beg to bother you, but that last group of White arrivals are causin' trouble." "Trouble! You say trouble? We never had no trouble here. Oh! What am I to do?" asked the Lord. St. Peter said, "Lord, if I may suggest, the only one who will know how to handle this matter is Mephistopheles. "No," said the Lord, "I can't ask him. We haven't been on good terms since I kicked his aah...him from up here, but what other choice do I have? Oh well! It's worth a try."

The Lord picked up the heavenly cell phone and dialed 1-800-HOT-FIRE. The phone rang in hell. The devil answered. "This is D, whutup?" "Devil, this is the Lord." "Who?" said the devil. "It's me, the Lord. I know that we haven't spoken for a while." "What do you want?" asked the devil, annoyed. "Devil, I need your help. I'm havin' trouble up here with White folks. I want to send them down there to you," said the Lord. "No! You can't send them here, I have my own problems with nigs—I mean African-Americans down here done put my fire out," said the devil. "Dr. King had a dream. We are havin' a nightmare. When the meek inherit the earth, they will have a mess on their hands."

# MESSAGE TO PARENTS

Now I want to confabulate with all you parents 'n' old folk here tonight. Sweetman is aware of 'n' sympathizes with your dilemma. Your offspring is causin' you to be fit to be tied. You are not alone. Parents all over the world are catchin' hell from their children. Even Miss Lizzy is in a tizzy. I speak of none other that Diana's former momma-in-law, her Royal Majesty, the Queen of Great Britain. She is fit to be tied as the fairy tale marriages of her dysfunctional prodigy, the fruit of her royal loins, has turned into "Tales From the Dark Side."

The Queen's oldest son, his Highness Charles, the Prince of Whales, slung his princely pecker like a commoner in the direction of every woman except his former wife, Princess Diana, causin' her to split from the House of Windsor, throwin' it into an uproar and causin' the Queen to suffer royal distraction.

In these days of selfishness and me, me, me, gimme, gimme, gimme, I want, blah, blah, blah it costs as much to pacify a child as it does to feed (oh how they can eat), clothe, and educate them. I often wonder what today's children will tell their children they had to do without. Many young people whoop 'n' holler about how they want to "git paid." Well, Sweetman has the answer for you, now listen up! If you are tired of listenin' to your stupid parents, here's what you do: Move out, get a job, pay your own bills, and hurry up while you still know everything! Let me say this to you young people. You are goin' a long way in life. You better hurry up, midnight's comin'. Sometimes some of you parents look at you offspring and think to yourselves, What was I thinking? Well, it's too late now.

Today parents have their hands full. Just to get your child ready for school is a chore. You have to make sure that they are equipped with survival gear: Gas mask, pit bull repellent, bullet proof vest, mace and condoms. Then pray they don't get food poisoning from the school lunch, or worse, some crazed teacher don't run off and elope with them, or they don't fall prey to freaks and drug dealers.

I've got to say this because it makes my long johns gather betwix my lower quarters when I hear some parents 'n' old folk goin' 'roun talkin' crazy talk 'bout how entertainers—Boxers (bite each other), singers, rappers, TV and movie stars, dancers, moon walkers, and other celebrities—should be role models for their children.

An entertainer is an entertainer, no more, no less; however if they happen to be "wrapped tight" and present a positive example, that's good. Parents, it's your job to raise and be good role models for your children, not entertainers who in most cases aren't much older or are the same age as their children. So take responsibility for your children. Don't wait until the TV announcer asks, "It's ten o'clock. Do you know where your children are?" Then you hop up 'n' holler, "Where are the kids?"

If you're plannin' on gettin' rich, don't have children. Young people are slicker than grease. Even if they have a job, they will still spend your money 'n' keep theirs.

A twelve-year-old girl threatened to run away from home. "How soon will you be leavin'?" asked her mother. "As soon as I can pack," the girl answered. "Here, let me help you," said the mother. A six-year-old boy came home from school all excited, "Daddy, daddy, guess what?" "What?" asked the father. "I learned how to do magic in school today. Do you want to see me make something disappear?" "Yes, let me see you make yourself disappear," the father said. In these crazy times, children grow up fast. A twelve-year-old boy said to his seven-year-old brother, "I found a condom in big brother's jogging suit." "What's a jogging suit?" asked the seven year old.

Today's young people dress funny, act funny, and talk funny. Ask them to do something, they will look at you funny and ask, "Is you illin'?" A fourteen year old boy said to his father, "Yo pops, my birthday is next week 'n' I need some stupid money, so I can get funky fresh." I ask you, what kind of talk is that? Umph, umph, umph!

Another thing, young people are gold crazy. I read in the newspaper last week that all the gold is missin' from Fort Knox. No one seems to kno' where it is. It's in the hip-hoppa's mouth. I saw a young hip-hoppa leanin' up against his jeep. He had a mouth full of gold teeth and a pit bull on a leash. The dog had gold teeth in it's mouth. Both of them were grinnin' like two fools; it looked as though their mouths were on fire. A young boy got mugged last week. The mugger didn't take nothin' but his teeth. The boy was last seen sittin' in McDonald's, tryin' to gum a Big Mac.

Now if this ain't a bitch 'n' two fruit cakes: A young man went into a jewelry store; he had gold rings on all ten fingers. He asked the jeweler to let him see some rings. The jeweler looked at his fingers and said, "Excuse me, but where are you going to put them?" The young man unzipped his pants 'n' dropped his drawers, umph!

Suddenly, Sweetman stopped, rolled his eyes and licked his lips and dabbed them with his red handkerchief. Zig-zagging from the subject at hand, he broke into laughter. We were all waiting for what was to come next. Knowing Sweetman, it would be something from out of left field.

Ha, ha, ha...Oh my, I'm reminded of a story. One hot summer day, a woman was sitting at the kitchen table with her legs ajar, wearing no under garments because it was such a hot day she wanted her quarters to get some air. Her six-year-old son was playin' on the floor and suddenly looked up betwix his mother's members. "What is that, mommy?", pointing betwix his mother's quarters. "Oh son, that's my face cloth," the mother explained. A week later the weather was much cooler, so she had her underwear on, sittin' with her legs ajar. The boy was playin' on the floor. He looked up betwixt his mother's limbs 'n' said, "Mommy, what happened to your face cloth?" "Oh son, I lost it." The child jumped up from the floor 'n' said, "Mommy, I'm goin' to find your face cloth." Before the mother could call the child back 'n' explain, he was out of the apartment. About ten minutes later, the boy rushed back into the apartment all out of breath (you would be out of breath too, if you saw what he saw). "Mommy, mommy, I found your face cloth. The lady on the third floor is washing daddy's face with it." Umph! There ain't no tellin' what kind of ruttish notions was stirred up in that child. Older people should be careful of what they do 'n' say in the presence of youngens.

On a sad note, with the ever escalation of drugs 'n' violence, children are leavin' this world at an alarming rate. Not long ago, a young drug dealer was struck down. At his wake, his cellular phone rang in his casket, 'rousin' the mourners from their grief. That's one call he didn't answer. The Lord said, "Suffer little children to come unto me." I kno' he would like to say to some of them, "Git thee hence!"

One day, the Lord was kicked back havin' a quiet day in heavenly peace, after he had settled that troublin' matter regardin' the White folks, listenin' to the soothin' sounds of harp music 'n' the voices of the celestial choir. Without warnin', the peace 'n' calm was shattered by the ungodly sound of Jeeps 'n' boom boxes blarin' at full volume. The Lord jumped up 'n' said, "St. Peter, go hither and see what is causin' this hellish tintinnabulation." St. Peter hurried forth, looked out of the Pearly Gates, and beheld Biggie Smalls, Tupac Shakur, 'n' a Crew of hip-hoppas a comin' across the clouds toward the sanctuary of the Lord. "Lord! Lordy Lord! Something called hip-hoppas are coming." "Hip-hoppa? What's a hip-hoppa?" asked the Lord, taken-a-back. "Children, loud, funky-fresh children," said St. Peter. The Lord mused for a moment. "Well, I did say, 'suffer little children to come unto me', but I didn't realize that they would be coming this fast. I've given my word. Go let them in." "Word up!" said St. Peter.

# COMMUNICATION

Clear communication is vital in these times of high technology if we're to avoid miscommunication, which breeds misunderstanding. Therefore, it's incumbent upon communicants to communicate in a concise manner when communing with others. I'm quite disturbed when I hear newscasters or media personalities violate this sacred principle of communication and scatterate the oberlum. or profferlate the scatelattor, making the information they're divulging loquacious. This multiloquous trait is ubiquitous among today's hi-tech communicators the world over, whose lips move faster than the wings of a fruit fly in Philly. For instance, some newscasters will engage in a scatteracious oberlum and embellish a simple statement like, "Good evening".

The twenty-first century is upon us: Ebonics my ass! We are living in a high-tech society riddled with low-tech minds. Therefore, it is essential that today's youth (of every race) are well educated. Students must realize that hip-hop won't qualify them for a job in a doughnut shop.

Take it from me, they can't get a degree watching MTV. Many of today's high school students as well as college graduates have tremendous difficulty profferlatting the English language. They'll trip a noun and hark a pronoun and won't know the difference. For instance, they'll trip a verb and have an assanatious understanding of an adverb and look at you with a doggansious look on their faces if you dare correct them. I've seen students take a test and become confused by the horker-mattus right before them. This is understandable, however, when we take into account the fact that many of today's young teachers aren't capable of strapperlating the horker-mattus, so the students end up with a flabberacious understanding of the curriculum. It's frightening when you consider how many people who can't read or write are driving automobiles . They'll skiddlelop a traffic sign and lolycomme a nagel on a one-way street, then pitch-a-bitch 'n' cuss you out if you toot your horn. They're subject to jump out of their car 'n' buss a cap up in yo' ass, 'cause you tried to warn them of impending doom, to you and themselves.

In my simple opinion, simplification of communication is of a vital necessity if we as human beings are to humblelate the oberlum with one another in a luciferous manner, thus allowing for a more friendly and harmonious atmosphere to prevail in today's multicultural society. Understandably, since clear and simplified communication is not compendious among the various races of people throughout the world, the multiglobal community is faced with racial mistrust, misunderstanding, misjudgment and misgiving, which in turn bring about misinterpretation, compelling us to rain tons of missiles up each other's asses.

I, The Sweetman, bein' one who is not well lettered, however, is of the opinion that today's racial conflicts are the fideicommissum that we are heir to, left to us by our forefathers (or masters); but through epigrammatic dialogue and synoptic communication, Black and White people can proffilate the obloum with each other, putting the past and bad blood that exists between us behind us, causing racism to become extinct and the desire to kick each other's asses to abate.

I feel that world peace would be within our reach if we were to take this process a step further and strabberlate the Italiano with the Italians, ying-yang with the Chinese, Ien glubber un ihken snoller vixen glurber with the

Germans 'n' mida mida wit' da Puerto Ricans 'n' partake of a bowl of chicken soup 'n' Cyberseder with our Jewish brethren 'n' what not. I feel certain that others would follow our lead, so-forth-'n'-so-on...Whew!

The communication (print/electronic) community must join our effort. My feelings are stringent in this regard, because many of their members are experts at negative sound bites and masters at twisting words and distorting images, like a poison ivy vine entwined 'round a tree trunk, causin' all who come in contact with it to break out in a rash of confusion, misperception, misconception, misunderstanding, hugger-mugger, and what not.

"What in hell is Sweetman talking about," someone said out loud. "Ask yo' momma," Sweetman shot back as he continued his blathskite. The media-the twisters 'n' manipulators of images are clever wordmongers 'n' phrasemeisters who can talk the smile off of a baby's face and make their listeners, viewers, and readers believe that a buzzard is a turkey, never mind that the buzzard is feasting on carrion 'n' the turkey on corn. There's no end to their chicanery. These (some) masters of misinformation are fully sentient of the fact that the majority of their listeners, readers, 'n' viewers aren't capable of analytical thought and will seize upon almost anything that is presented to them in a glib and persuasive fashion.

Some of today's media icons, with impunity, play the 'distortion card', dealing the public a hand from the bottom of the deck of misinformation, which perpetually feed stereotypical images, ideas, and notions, which can lead to mulligatawny—you know damned well that can be a bitchy batch of bitches bitching without their britches in Britain. As a nation we must meet (as President Clinton has said), "upon common ground." And I say, either that, or we will find ourselves standing on sinking sand and our asses in mud up to our necks. Common ground must be sought for the common good of the common man. A peaceful community, city, state, or nation is one that is grounded in good communication and racial harmony. Their members strappulate the horkums with each other and are therefore free of misunderstanding, which erodes and undermines racial relationships. Don't you agree? Racism. What is it? I'll tell you what it is—foolishness! Foolishness that has bred all the ills of the world. This asininity is born out of the notion that God favors one race of people or religion over the other. Nonsense! Bull cookies! Horsefruit! The Almighty would not be able to tell the difference between the various peoples of the earth because they all look alike to Him, Her, It—whatever—because they are all a part of the great whole, Life!

Example: A piano has black and white keys, and notes that range from the very low to the very high pitched, yet they harmonize in unison to make music. God does not have a favorite anything, people or otherwise. I invite you to study 'n' observe life's multivarious forms 'n' you will conclude that this simple statement proves that the point I'm trying to make is the truth, unless of course, you are educated to the point of stupidity. There too, are those among you who will say that I have committed blasphemy or worst. To you I say what I said to that preacher in Chicago. Do you remember what that was? It'll come to you.

When The Sweetman points out to you the issues of life that confront you in a poignant manner, some of you become quite annoyed with me and say, "Oh, Sweetman is crazy and two pieces of lunch meat short of a sandwich." Any fool, from Flatbush to Florida, who has full sight can see that the strife that exists today amongst the peoples of the earth is caused by poisoned thinkin', misunderstandin', 'n' scrappernacious miscommunication. Let me give you an example of synoptic communication 'n' good will.

On Sunday mornings, week after week, the residents of Harlem are 'roused from their Sunday morning slumber by the most ungodly noise, the rumblin' of tour buses that sound like an invasion of Sherman tanks, ferrying White people to the various Black churches in Harlem to see a show—oops—I mean, they come to Harlem on Sunday mornings to take photographs—oops, here I go again. What's wrong with me? What I mean to say is, White folks from all over flock to Harlem on Sunday mornings to partake in Black church services—"Yeah right"—my tongue, my tongue! Why do thou runnith amuck? Umph!

Well, anyway, I feel that this is a good thing that White people come to Harlem for spiritual comfort. An idea dawned upon me not long ago: Contact Reverend Al Sharpton and the Venerable Jesse Jackson. Both have the ability to organize large numbers of Black people at the drop of a dollar bill in the collection plate after a fiery sermon. They could organize a contingent of Harlemmites 'n' shepherd them onto tour buses 'n' sally forth on Sunday mornin' 'n' pay a visit to the White churches over in Bensonhurst (Brooklyn, N.Y.) and Howard Beach (Queens, N.Y.) so that Black Christian folk' from Harlem could Tabernacle 'n' what-not with our White Christian bretheren 'n' sisteren; like they come to watch, ah, Tabernacle with us here in Harlem.

Let us take this reachin' out 'n' Tabernaclin' a step further if you will. The good Reverends could also extend the lovin' arm of Black Christian fellowship to our Hasidic Brethren out yonder in Crown Heights (Brooklyn, N.Y.), encouragin' them to hoist the lovin' cup of Jewish fellowship with us here in Harlem. This Christian 'n' Jewish outreach 'n' what-not should not present a problem to Reverend Sharpton, due to the fact that he is well known to, and is acquainted with all three of these White communities. This is an interestin' idea, don't you think? Well...

Bein' a man of a longanimous nature, it is not my intent to stir the nefarious winds of racial rancor, rather, my intent is to suggest, if you will, a way to temper, put a damper on, the ill-natured feelings that have long existed between the Black 'n' White communities throughout the country.

If this plan could be instituted, the Nobel Peace Prize would be bestowed upon Reverend Al Sharpton and those involved in this endeavor, umph! I should be workin' for the United Nations. How do I come up with these brilliant ideas?

# EPILOGUE

*S*weetman pauses...mops his brow. His expression suddenly changes from one that was a moment ago wild, wacky and witty, to one that is now halcyon and unfathomable. It seemed as though he is on the verge of metamorphosis. His speech becomes quickened, his physical being altered....Ray Charles was singing in the background...*O beautiful for spacious skies, for amber waves of grain; for purple mountain majesty, above the fruited plane ....*

Well, well, well, Sweetman continues his largiloquence. As most of you kno' by now I'm not given to bein' syllabus, but I must, for my hour of departure draweth nigh 'n' The Sweetman cannot tarry with you much longer. But befo' I go, I want you to kno' that I'm fully aware of the nonsense that you are bombarded with from every quarter of life. This is why I try to pull yo' coat, however some of you have to be stripped naked. Even then, unclothed, buck naked, with yo' hidden parts exposed to the world, you look befuddled 'n' cry, "I don't understand!" As you catch cold in yo'—good grief people, wake up! Git hip, git a grip 'n' git to gittin' befo' it's too late. Stop gittin' side tracked, high jacked, 'n' taken for a ride, boat or otherwise. People, wake up and think! That's why you got a brain.

Keep yo' mind on yo' own affairs. Stop worryin' 'bout Madonna's baby, Murphy Brown's baby, and Michael Jackson's baby (umph! Lord have mercy!). Take care of yo' own baby 'n' pray that Rosemary don't give birth to another baby. I beseech you to cleave unto my words.

Verily I say unto you, laughter is a healin' balm that is beneficial to one's emotional and spiritual well-being, especially in these times of ugliness, which doesn't give one much to cachinnate about. That's why I ride into Jerusalem—oops....I mean Harlem—every seven years with the Spring zephyr to inform as well as to make you titter, snicker, snigger, sniggle 'n' giggle, yuckle 'n' chuckle, bus'-a-gut 'n' what-not.

From what I've seen, I arrived none too soon, 'cause some of you haven't laughed in so long, you are down right ugly. Yo' brow has mo' ridges than a' old fashioned wash board. Yo' face look like forty-eight miles of rough road. Yo' lips are as tight as a horse's hiney.

Therefore, my yoke fellows, befo' I sally forth into the night, let me say, just as government cheese will lock yo' bowels, pride will lock the door to knowledge 'n' prevent you from benefitin' from my Fools Guide For Livin'. If I have vexed you, caused you to have a cat-fit 'n' take exception to my pungent circumrambledge this evening, don't sweat it or let it throw you into high dudgeon, but rather take my drollery as a challenge 'n' go forth from this hollowed house 'n' share my missive wit' yo' misses, homies, yokies, 'n' what-not. And to those of you whose intellection has allowed you to grasp the pith of my puissant prissology, I thank you for yo' placification (for the last time, you know what to do). And those of you whom I've offended, I stand chasten and rebuked. Until I come again—peace!

*Tu Tu Na Na!*

# FADE TO BLACK

*T*he pre-dawn silence is shattered. Quiet on the set! Roll camera! Action!" Like in Crystal Streams flowing, a torrent of tears cascaded down my face as Spike Lee's 40 Acres 'N' A Mule Filmworks got a close-up of Sweetman's ass as it disappeared into the darkness. Then turning to face the camera, I said: Sweetman is like a breath of Spring in the wilderness of hugger-mugger and uncertainty.... "Cut!! That's a wrap!"

# FINIS

*Photo: Clayborne Thomas, NY*